BELGIUM

Unity of diversity

A COUNTRY CAN NEVER BE SMALL WHEN IT BORDERS ON THE SEA.

LEOPOLD II, KING OF THE BELGIANS
(1835 - 1909)

BELGIUM

Unity of diversity

With contributions from:

PHILIPPE BODSON

Chairman of the Confederation of Belgian
Industry

ETIENNE DAVIGNON

Former Ambassador

JOHAN FLEERACKERS

Chairman of the Permanent Supervisory
Committee for Language Matters

ANDRE MOLITOR

Honorary Principal Private Secretary to the
King

WALTER PREVENIER

Professor of Medieval History at the State
University of Ghent

PHILIPPE ROBERTS-JONES

Permanent Secretary of the Belgian Royal
Academy of Science, Literature and the
Arts

HERMAN VAN DER WEE

Professor of Social and Economic History
at the Catholic University of Louvain

lannoo

The publishers would like to thank the Ministry of Foreign Affairs, Foreign Trade and Development Cooperation, the Belgian Department of Foreign Trade, the Directorate General for Development Cooperation, the Confederation of Belgian Industry, the Belgisch Instituut voor Voorlichting en Documentatie (Belgian Institute of Information and Documentation) and the many institutes, companies and individuals who have contributed in any way whatsoever to the conception and production of this book.

Typeset, printed and bound by
Drukkerij-Uitgeverij Lannoo bvba, Tielt,
Belgium - 1987
© Uitgeverij Lannoo
Printed in Belgium
ISBN 90 209 1489 8
D/1987/45/113

Graphic design by
Bureau Fiszman + Partners
(Johanna Fischer)

Photos on dust-jacket:
Philip Vanoutrive, Christine Bastin &
Jacques Evrard, Jan Decreton,
Philip Vanoutrive, Philip Vanoutrive,
Christine Bastin & Jacques Evrard.

Translation
E.L. Dijkstra-Tucker

This book is published simultaneously in four editions:

The Dutch and English editions by
Uitgeverij Lannoo, Tielt, Belgium

The French edition by
Les Editions Duculot, Gembloux, Belgium

The German edition by
Grenz-Echo Verlag, Eupen, Belgium

CONTENTS

IT IS CLEAR THAT WHILE THE DIVERSITY OF THE CULTURES ALIVE IN BELGIUM
MAY SOMETIMES BE A SOURCE OF FRICTION,
THIS SAME DIVERSITY CAN AND MUST ALSO BE ABOVE ALL
A SOURCE OF SPIRITUAL AND MATERIAL ENRICHMENT.

FOR THIS VERY REASON, AND BECAUSE BELGIUM IS THE COMMON GROUND
WHERE TWO GREAT EUROPEAN CULTURES MEET,
WE MUST CONTINUE TO BE WHAT WE HAVE ALWAYS BEEN IN THE PAST:
PIONEERS IN THE CONSTRUCTION OF A UNITED EUROPE.

KING BAUDOUIN

in a Christmas broadcast on radio and television in 1986.

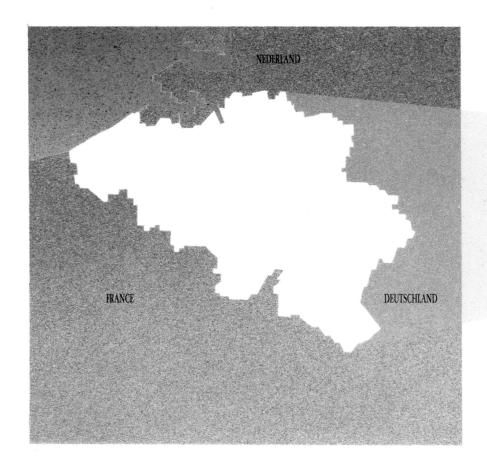

GEOGRAPHY

Belgium covers an area of 30,518 km^2. Of this, 45.5 % is agricultural land and 19.5 %, mainly in the south-east, is woodland. Two important rivers run through the country from south to north: the Meuse and the Scheldt, with a catchment area of 13,300 km^2 and 15,000 km^2 respectively.
The relief varies from 0.05 m to 649 m above the average sea level at low tide.

CLIMATE

With the exception of the higher regions of the Ardennes, Belgium enjoys a moderate maritime climate under the influence of the warm Gulf Stream and the prevailing west and south-west winds.
The coldest month of the year is January, with an average temperature of 2.6°C. The warmest month is July, with an average temperature of 17.1°C.

POPULATION

On 1 Jaunary 1986, a total of 9,859,000 Belgians was counted. In addition, nearly 800,000 foreigners from all corners of the world now also live in Belgium. The fact that so many multi-nationals — and the Commission of the European Economic Community — have set up their headquarters in Belgium, has of course contributed to this evolution. This international community feels at home in Belgium. A variety of international schools, organizations, clubs and in Brussels even an English-language magazine have been established. There are three national languages in Belgium. Dutch is spoken in Brussels and Flanders. Flanders accounts for 57.7 % of the total population of Belgium. French is spoken by a majority of the inhabitants of Brussels and by the inhabitants of Wallonia, which represents 31.9 % of the Belgian population. The bilingual City of Brussels area houses 9.9 % of the population, while 0.7 % live on the German-speaking region. The majority of Belgians are Roman Catholic. But Belgium maintains a high degree of tolerance, and religious freedom is one of the rights guaranteed in the Constitution. The Roman Catholic, Protestant-evangelical, Anglican, Jewish and Islamic religions are recognised by the state.
The Belgian birth rate is low (11.59 %), but the average life-expectancy is high: 70 years for men and 77 for women.

NATIONAL ANTHEM

The 'Brabançonne', the Belgian national anthem, was created in the wake of the events which led to Belgian Independence in 1830. The text of the first version was written by an actor at the Théatre de la Monnaie, Louis-Alexandre Dechet, under the pseudonym of Jenneval. François Van Campenhout, a violinist at the same theatre, composed the music and gave it a title.

NATIONAL FLAG

On 23 January 1831, the Provisional Government adopted the heraldic colours of the old Duchy of Brabant — black, yellow and red — as the colours of Belgium.

COAT OF ARMS

The Belgian coat of arms is dominated by the Belgian Lion, a heraldic symbol found in our region since the XIth century. It is said to have been brought back from the Middle East by the Crusaders, and is found in most coats of arms, including those of all the Belgian provinces except Antwerp.
Both coats of arms bear the national motto: 'Eendracht maakt macht' - United we stand.

A PARLIAMENTARY MONARCHY

Belgium is a democratic constitutional state, with elected representatives and a hereditary monarchy. Legislative power is exercised by the two chambers of parliament and the King. The ministers hold executive power, headed by the King. Judicial power is exercised by the courts and tribunals.

Since 1970, the central government has devolved part of its powers to the Communities and the Regions. The people of Belgium enjoy many rights, including the right to vote from the age of 18. The Constitution prescribes that all Belgians are equal before the law and guarantees the freedom of the individual, freedom of speech and therefore also freedom of the press and religious freedom in Belgium, as well as freedom of language.

SOURCES: het Belgisch Instituut voor Voorlichting en Documentatie (Belgian Institute of Information and Documentation), the Ministry of Internal Affairs and the Ministry of Foreign Affairs, Foreign Trade and Development Cooperation.

ROMAN COLONISATION

57 BC: During his campaign in Gaul, Caesar overcame the Nervii and the Aduatuci.

51 BC: Roman colonisation begins with the surrender of the Eburones and the Treveri.

27 BC: Augustus divides Gaul into *Gallia togata* (or *provincia*) and *Gallia comata*. The Belgic province was part of the latter.

THE GERMANIC INVASIONS

Towards the middle of the 3rd century AD, the first wave of Franks, Saxons and Frisians invaded Belgic territory.

Around the year 350 came the first christianisation of towns and cities: the bishopric of Tongres was constituted in the year 343.

Around 450, virtually the whole of Belgic territory was under Frankish rule: Chlovis was residing at Tournai.

UNDER THE MEROVINGIANS AND THE CAROLINGIANS

During the 6th and 7th centuries, under the Merovingians, Belgic territory lay on the borders of the Frankish kingdoms of Neustria and Austrasia.

Towards the middle of the 8th century, under the Pippinides and later under Charlemagne, the Meuse region became an essential pivot of the Carolingian kingdom.

843 AD: The river Scheldt became a frontier under the Treaty of Verdun: the territories west of the river (which later became the Country of Flanders) went to Charles the Bald; those east of the river went to Lothar and became known as Lotharingia.

THE TERRITORIAL PRINCIPALITIES AND THE TOWNS

925 AD: Lotharingia was attached to Germania. The Scheldt became a frontier between France and Germany.

Various principalities emerged in Lotharingia, forming virtually autonomous units whithin the Empire: Liège, Brabant and Hainaut.

In Flanders, the Count's authority supplanted that of the King of France, especially as Flemish economic interests caused Flanders to turn towards England.

THE BURGUNDIAN PERIOD

1384: Philip the Bold, Duke of Burgundy (1364-1404) received Flanders and Artois from his father-in-law although he remained a vassal of the King of France. His son John the Fearless (1404-1419) took the lead in the Burgundian faction that favoured the English.

Philip the Good (1419-1467), son of John the Fearless, increased the Burgundian estates by purchase, marriage and inheritance.

Under Charles the Rash (1467-1477), son of Philip the Good, the Liège region was laid waste on several occasions because 'it wanted none of Burgundy'.

UNDER THE HABSBURGS

1477: Mary of Burgundy, daughter of Charles the Rash, was married to Maximilian of Austria, later to become the Emperor.

1493: Philip the Handsome, son of Mary, became the overlord of the Low Countries. In 1496 he married Joanna, heiress of the sovereign rulers of Aragon and Castile. From then on, the fate of the Low Countries was linked to the House of Spain.

1506: Charles, son of Philip, who was born in Ghent, received the Low Countries and later inherited the kingdoms of Spain; he was elected Emperor of the Holy Roman Empire in 1519. He gave the Low Countries a centralised government with a Council of State, a Privy Council and a Finance Council.

SPANISH RULE

Philip II, Regent from 1543 on, continued the policies of his father Charles V. In 1559 he handed the government of the Low Countries to Margaret of Parma, his illegitimate half-sister.

1567: The Duke of Alba was appointed Governor of the Low Countries with orders to stamp out heresy by every means.

In 1595 Philip II entrusted the government of the Low Countries to Archduke Albert, sixth son of Maximilian II. In 1598 Albert married his cousin Isabella, daughter of Philip II, who brought him the Low Countries as her dowry.

1635: War of conquest undertaken by the Dutch in the Southern Netherlands.

1648: Spain ceded Northern Brabant and Zeeland Flanders to the United Provinces.

1659-1678: Spain relinquished Artois and parts of Flanders and Hainaut to France.

1713: The Treaty of Utrecht gave the Spanish Netherlands to Austria.

AUSTRIAN RULE

The Austrian rulers were at pains to encourage prosperity in the Southern Netherlands: the road network was modernised, the death rate fell. The country was by now one of the most densely populated in Europe: 100 inhabitants per square kilometer in Brabant and in Flanders.

Walloon industry was in full expansion: coalmines, metallurgy, glass and textiles.

In the name of enlightened despotism, Charles VI (1711-1740) and Maria Theresa (1740-1780) curtailed the prerogatives of the clergy, restricted the spread of convents, and levied taxes on church property.

1781: Joseph II (1780-1790) was determined to reduce the Catholic clergy solely to its religious function by signing the Edict of Tolerance. The clergy came entirely under State control (Josephism).

FRENCH RULE

1792: The Emperor's intervention in the war against revolutionary France brought the Low Countries into the conflict. The victory of Dumouriez at Jemappes on 6 November forced the Austrians to evacuate Belgium.

The French defeat at Neerwinden on 18 March 1793 brought the Austrians back again.

After the victory of Fleurus on 26 June 1794, France annexed the Austrian Netherlands, the Liège region and the territories ceded by a vanquished Holland.

1815: On 18 June at Waterloo, the fate of the French Empire was finally settled.

THE KINGDOM OF THE NETHERLANDS

21 July 1814: The Allies — especially England — who were determined to set up a 'barrier' to contain France, decided upon the principle of a Kingdom of the Netherlands that would comprise the United Provinces, the former Austrian Netherlands, and the ecclesiastical principality of Liège.

16 March 1815: The Kingdom of the Netherlands was set up with the Prince of Orange as its ruler, who became King William I.

An heir of the 'enlightened despots' of the 18th century, William I secured the support of many Belgian industrialists by his policy of economic dirigism, but he also aroused the opposition of the Catholics and the Walloons by enacting tactless laws in the matter of language, the press and religion (the clergy accused him of narrow Calvinism and Josephism). The Catholics, concerned with the freedom of education, and the Liberals (often anti-clerical) who were concerned with the freedom of the press, joined forces (unionism) in opposition to the King.

Inspired by the July Revolution in France, the Belgians rose in rebellion in Brussels (25 August), drove out the Dutch troops (27 September), proclaimed the separation of North and South (29 September) and the full independence of Belgium (4 October).

THE KINGDOM OF BELGIUM

On 3 November 1830 the National Congress, elected by a direct ballot based on the property assessment, differential and qualification system, met to frame a Constitution.

On 20 January 1831 the London Conference, which had been in session since 4 November 1830, recognised the independence of Belgium and guaranteed the integrity and inviolability of her territory, bounded on the northern side by the old frontier of 1790.

On 7 Februari 1831 the National Congress ratified the Constitution, which was promulgated on 11 February.

The National Congress rejected the terms proposed by the London Conference with regard to Belgium's eastern and northern boundaries. Preliminary

peace talks (26 June 1831), also known as the *Eighteen Articles*, left the question of further negotiations open with regard to the contested territories.

Leopold of Saxe-Coburg, the widower of an English princess, accepted the crown on condition that Congress should ratify the Eighteen Articles. He took the Constitutional Oath on 21 July 1831.

On 2 August 1831 the Dutch invaded Belgium. France came to the latter's help.

In 1838-1839 the Dutch ended by accepting the independence of Belgium, on which a status of perpetual neutrality was imposed.

LÉOPOLD I

The reign of Léopold I was characterised by the development and organization of the Belgian State. Provincial and Municipal Laws were passed in April 1836, and the Liberals (in 1846) and the Catholics (around 1860) organized themselves into political parties. The first railway in continental Europe was opened between Brussels and Mechelen on 5 May 1835, a symbol of the process of industrialization and renewal which was to make Belgium a leading industrial nation.

LÉOPOLD II

King Léopold II ascended the throne on 17 December 1865. With the abolition in 1866 of the coalition ban, which dated from the time of the French rule, the way was clear for the rise of the labour movement. The first language laws concerning the use of the Dutch language in criminal proceedings and administrative matters were passed in 1873 and 1878 respectively. The Equality Act of 1898 put French *and* Dutch on an equal footing as the official languages of

Belgium. On 26 February 1885, the Conference of Berlin recognised the existence of the Congo Free State and the sovereignty of King Léopold over this territory, which was only officially accepted by the Belgian State as a colony in 1908.

ALBERT I

After the accession of Albert I on 23 December 1909, the international situation became more and more serious. The invasion by German troops on 4 August 1914 was a violation of Belgium's neutrality. The heroic resistance of the Belgian army and its allies on the front at the river IJzer succeeded in preventing the occupation of the whole of Belgium by the agressors. The treaty of Versailles assigned the German cantons of Eupen, Malmédy and Sankt-Vith to Belgium, as well as the administration of two provinces of the German colonies: Urundi and Ruanda. The Belgian commitment to remain neutral was abolished.

The second revision of the Constitution officially introduced universal single-vote male suffrage on 7 February 1921. And on 25 July 1921, the signature of the Belgium-Luxembourg Economic Union abolished customs barriers between the two countries.

The Language Act of June 1932 stated that Flanders was Dutch-speaking — not bilingual — and the subsequent Act of 14 July 1932 made the use of Dutch compulsory in both primary and secondary education in Flanders. Legal proceedings had to be conducted exclusively in Dutch in Flanders from 1935 onwards.

LÉOPOLD III

King Léopold III ascended the throne on 23 February 1934 in a period of economic crisis. From 1936, Belgium re-

verted to its policy of neutrality. In May 1940, the Belgian army capitulated to the German invaders, after a few weeks of heroic resistance. King Léopold opted to remain with his troops and spent the rest of the war as a prisoner of war. Part of the Government fled to London, where it formed a Government in exile from October 1940 onwards. In view of the imprisonment of the royal family, Prince Karel, the king's brother, was appointed Regent by the two chambers after the Liberation on 20 September 1944.

After the war, Belgium contributed on the foundation of the United Nations (26 June 1945), the Treaty of Brussels (17 March 1948), the North Atlantic Treaty Organization (4 April 1949) and the Council of Europe (5 May 1949).

KING BAUDOUIN

On 10 August 1950 the royal prerogatives were legally handed over to the crown prince, who was still in minor at the time, and the following day he took the constitutional oath as the prince royal.

Belgium signed the agreement setting up the European Coal and Steel Community (1951) and the treaty founding the European Economic Community and the European Atomic Energy Community (EURATOM) in 1957. European integration remained one of the pillars of Belgian foreign policy. The Belgian Congo became independent on 30 June 1960, followed by the dependent territories of Burundi and Ruanda on 1 July 1962.

The Act of 29 May 1959 ratified the school pact agreed between the three national parties representing the different philosophies. This pact was designed to guarantee freedom of choice in education, as laid down in the Constitution, by ensuring adequate provision

everywhere of both confessional and non-confessional schools.

In 1962 and 1963, acts were passed fixing the language frontier and the four linguistic areas. Tension between the two largest cultural communities in the country led to the division of all the national parties into independent French-language and Dutch-language parties. The constitutional reforms of 1970 and 1980 devolved wider cultural and economic powers to the 'Communities', with their mandate for matters concerning culture and the individual, and the 'Regions', with powers in the field of social and economic matters. This radical reorganization of the state will be completed during the coming years.

ROAD NETWORK

RIVERS AND CANALS

✈ AIRPORTS

SEAPORTS

☩ ABBEYS, MONASTERIES

■ RECREATION PARK

▢ CASTLE

RUINS

★ OTHER PLACES
OF INTEREST

⛷ SKI-RUN

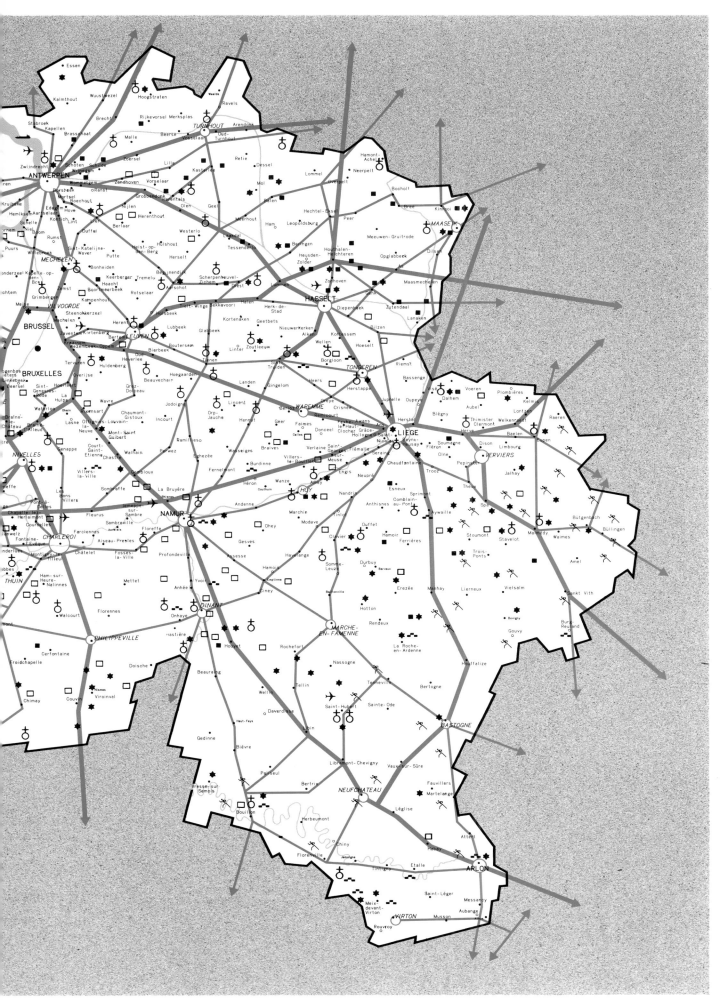

THE

ERRATA

Page: 8

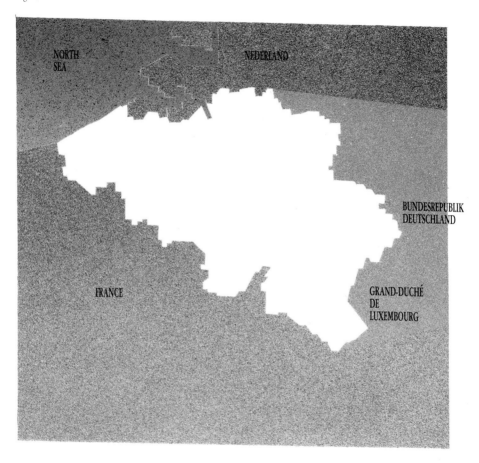

Page 19:
THE GERMAN COMMUNITY
read: THE GERMAN-SPEAKING COMMUNITY

Page 19:
THE FRENCH REGION
read: THE FLEMISH REGION

S T A T E

HISTORICAL FOUNDATIONS OF THE BELGIAN STATE UP TO 1830

WALTER PREVENIER

The provinces which, since 1830, formally constitute the state of Belgium also lived through periods before 1830 when they were united as the Low Countries under one ruler, but never in exactly the same combination as today. Sometimes Liège was included, and sometimes not. There were times when the Northern Low Countries (the Netherlands of today) and the Southern Low Countries were joined under one sceptre, for instance during the Burgundian period (15th-16th century) and under the United Kingdom of the Netherlands (1815-1830). Before and after these periods they functioned independently, but with close links with each other: the Benelux concept is the logical continuation of this today. One feature that stands out as a constant factor throughout the history of the Low Countries since the early Middle Ages is that they formed a politically sovereign or quasi-independent state or states which were frequently more prosperous and progressive than the rest of Europe in their time.

lowed their own economic policies. Philip of Alsace, Count of Flanders (1168-91), negotiated with the French and English kings on an equal footing. In 1204, Baldwin IX, Count of Flanders and Hainault, enjoyed such prestige that he was chosen as Emperor of the Holy Roman Empire by his fellow crusaders in Constantinople during the Fourth Crusade.

This desire for peaceful coexistence in the Low Countries, independent of the big powers, was stimulated in the first place by a very realistic sense of their own economic interdependence: luxury textiles in Flanders and Brabant, the metallurgical industry in Liège, and agriculture in Hainault and Luxembourg. The medieval inhabitants of the Low Countries had the extreme good fortune to live in a part of Europe which enjoyed a mild climate and a unique position on the estuaries of the great rivers. It was a golden delta, with excellent shipping links across the North Sea to the Baltic Sea and the Med-

iterranean, as well as good inland networks extending deep into France and Germany via the rivers, man-made canals and roads. The rich mineral resources of the area and the balanced relationship between agriculture and industry made it possible for about a third of the population to live in the towns, supported by supplies of foodstuffs produced by progressive agricultural techniques. All this meant that the Low Countries, together with Northern Italy, were the most highly urbanised area of Europe, where industry and commerce reached its peak earlier than in the rest of Europe. But the people of the Low Countries did not owe their solidarity to economic considerations alone. The art and culture they shared on a European scale, like the metalwork and sculpture of the Liège region, carved altarpieces from Brabant and the Flemish paintings of van Eyck and Memling, was an equally important factor binding the various territories together.

A sense of national identity crystallized in each of the principalities, in the first place around its own dynasty, but was also reflected in the formation of their own political, legal and financial institutions, and in symbolic, proud monuments: bell towers and town halls in Flanders and Hainault, and the perrons of Liège as symbols of its own judicial authority.

Whereas the regional rulers originally worked out their political decision making together with the nobility and the clergy, the growing urbanisation of the 12th century led to increasing political participation of the self-aware upper middle classes. The representation of the people gradually became almost entirely dominated by the towns. The representative bodies — the Provincial Estates of Flanders, Brabant etc. — constituted a real counterweight to the power of the princes and can be seen as a forerunner of our modern parliaments. However, we should not forget that democracy in the Middle Ages was

The Town Hall of Liège and its perron.

In the 9th century, the Low Countries were a small but economically prosperous and culturally active corner of the prestigious Carolingian Empire. When this political structure collapsed after 843, two great nations rose from the ruins in Northwest Europe: France and Germany. A number of smaller independent territories also emerged, on the lines of the former Carolingian territorial divisions, each with its own ruler: the Counties of Flanders, Hainault and Holland, the Duchy of Brabant, and the Prince-bishopric of Liège. Feudally and institutionally, these territories fell under the French crown (Flanders) or the German Emperor (the others), but their sovereignty was largely theoretical. In practice, the rulers of these territorial states conducted their own diplomatic relations with other countries and fol-

not as it is today, with power in the hands of a limited plutocracy. After a series of revolts around 1300, a broader spectrum of society won no more than a limited say in political matters. Nevertheless, the medieval citizens of Flanders, Brabant and Liège formulated in their byelaws a whole political deontology around the rights and duties of the prince, the protection of the individual and the right to a say in the government of the state — all of which, mutatis mutandis, heralded at least some of the tenets of the French Revolution. These same towns also made many attempts to dominate their hinterland, in defiance of their rulers, to set up city-states modelled on those of Italy.

When the Duke of Burgundy, Philip the Bold, married the only daughter of the Flemish count and became the new Count of Flanders in 1384, the threat to the independent political identity of Flanders looked very real. Philip was the son of the King of France and cherished ambitions in French national politics. But that is not the way it turned out. The strong awareness of a separate political and economic identity which had been built up over the ages both in Flanders and elsewhere in the Low Countries was in itself enough to discourage any attempts to undermine its independence. Moreover, the Dukes of Burgundy were soon to create a completely new set-up: the independent state of Burgundy, a state on a par with the traditional great powers of Europe. The territorial unification was largely completed by Duke Philip the Good (1419-64), for which Pontus Heuterus honoured him a century later with the title of 'imperii Belgici conditor'. But it would be naive to see this as heralding the Belgium of 1830. The intentions behind it were very different, and so was the geographical framework. In the 15th century, the Burgundian State in-

cluded both the Southern and the Northern Low Countries, and even Burgundy which today is part of France. The events of 1477 were proof of the continued existence of a sense of political identity in the Low Countries, and of the gradual acceptance of what was originally a foreign dynasty as their own dynasty. In 1477, the sudden death of Duke Charles the Bold offered France an opportunity to annex the Duchy of Burgundy. But despite the fact that the central figure and bearer of the name of the Duchy had gone, the Dukes of Burgundy continued to rule over the Low Countries as a whole, without anyone feeling a need to change the name, and without any moves by foreign nations to annex the northern part of the Burgundian State.

Although the Burgundian Low Countries gathered momentum again and developed into a national state after the restoration of authority after 1477, chance factors diverted the course of history in a quite different direction. Philip the Fair (1493-1506) married the crown princess of Spain and acceded to the Spanish throne, and Charles V (1515-55) inherited not only Spain (including the New World) but also his grandfather's German Empire in 1520. But in spite of the high prestige of this small country with its flourishing economy and art of European standing, it was inevitable that the relative importance of the land of his birth would fade for the central ruler in the wider context of his new possessions. International diplomacy in the new Hapsburg state was too sophisticated and complex for the Low Countries to be able to make a contribution of any real significance. In practice, the Low Countries were governed more and more by Madrid, especially under Philip II (1555-98), although governors were sent to Brussels to smooth over

the roughest edges of the Spanish rule.

However, this form of government was a complete failure. In the second half of the 16th century, a violent revolt erupted in the Low Countries against what had gradually come to be seen as the Spanish occupation and the despotism of Philip II. The revolt gained another dimension when a great number of the rebels took up the Protestant faith, which gave them yet another reason to chafe against the yoke of Catholic Spain. After many fluctuations in the course of the war, the curtain finally fell, almost by chance, in 1585. Antwerp was recaptured by the Spanish forces and the rebels retreated to the north of the great rivers, and this was to remain the final frontier, since both parties refrained from further attacks.

The north then went its own way as a sovereign state with its own stadholder: the United Provinces, later the Kingdom of the Netherlands. The south, or what was later Belgium, but without Liège, remained under the Spanish crown. It survived as a semi-independent province because the Spanish crown was represented by governors who enjoyed a certain amount of political freedom and who, like Albrecht and Isabella (1598-1621), were accepted more or less as native rulers, as in the past. But the emigration of many businessmen and intellectuals to the north was still a serious drain on human resources. Because of its strategic position as an outpost of Catholicism, the Spanish Low Countries evolved once again into a passive instrument in the hands of a Junta ruling from Madrid, as in the time of Philip II.

The long war of succession around the Spanish crown, and the ambition of England and the United Provinces to set up a new political balance of power in Europe, forced Spain to hand over

the Southern Low Countries to Austria in 1715. During the first decades of their rule, the Austrians proved to be even more despotic than Spain, and the role of the people's representative bodies was reduced to almost nothing. The crown was formally represented in the Low Countries by governors, but the actual business of policymaking was carried out by Ministers with a full mandate, who built up the process of government into an autocratic, modern streamlined bureaucracy.

However, from about 1750 onwards, the influence of the Enlightenment began to make itself felt, especially in the arts and education, and giving a new stimulus to the representative bodies. International trade and the capital market of Antwerp, too, gained a new impetus.

The Revolt of 1789 against Austria fizzled out, but in 1792 (and for the last time in 1794), the Austrian occupation was exchanged for the French. Institutions on the pattern of those in revolutionary France were introduced. The dynamic industrial and commercial middle classes made the Southern Low Countries the second country after England to achieve the Industrial Revolution, with a new stimulus for the textile industry in Flanders, and the metallurgical and coal industries in Wallonia.

In 1815, the Napoleonic Empire collapsed. The Congress of Vienna, in an attempt to prevent the enactment of yet more imperialistic scenarios, weighed up the balance of power in Europe with painstaking care and decided to unite the Northern and Southern Low Countries to form the United Kingdom of the Netherlands (1815-30) under King William I. But this construction did not survive long, in spite of its medieval antecedents. Since the Middle Ages, North and South had evolved in

THE INSTITUTIONS: FROM 1830 TO THE PRESENT DAY

ANDRÉ MOLITOR

different directions, and now had little in common. In addition to this cultural gap, there was also the religious gulf between the Protestant North and the Catholic South, and the French-speaking South was apprehensive of a predominantly Dutch-speaking state. The revolt of August and September 1830 established an independent state of Belgium.

The fact that Belgium, and the Southern Low Countries before it, were not swallowed up by any of the surrounding nations can probably be explained by the consideration that it would not have been in the interests of any of these larger nations for one of them to gain control of this strategically important area. But this implied that the area had to remain small politically, and therefore not a potential threat to any of its neighbours.

In the summer of 1830, the Belgian provinces of the Kingdom of the Netherlands rose up against the central governing authority for reasons described elsewhere, chief among which was the claim of oppression. Their declaration of independence brought Belgium as we know it today into being, and its existence was recognized — not without reluctance — by the neighbouring powers. In 1831, a National Congress endowed the fledgling state with its Constitution, granting Belgians a large measure of civil liberties in many areas of life — the same freedoms, indeed, which today form the common heritage of western democracies.

The new State was both unitary and decentralized: local authorities (provinces and municipalities) were granted extensive powers of self-government under the overall control of central government. The State took the form of a hereditary, constitutional monarchy, subject to Parliamentary authority and incorporating the principle of ministerial accountability to Parliament. The legislature is bi-cameral: the House of Representatives and the Senate, with equivalent powers. The judicial system — courts and tribunals — is, both in law and in fact, separate from the other powers.

The 1831 Constitution, which enshrined our ancient traditions and was modelled on the contemporary British and French examples, was highly advanced for its time, serving as a model for the fundamental laws of many other countries. It remained substantially unchanged until 1970 except in one respect: enfranchisement. The right to vote, initially the sole preserve of a small elite of wealthy citizens, was gradually extended until, in the 20th century, the principle of universal suffrage was recognized. But the constitution is framed with such flexibility as to allow the spirit of the law to progress within the letter. Its basis remains unaltered, but political practice has changed, sometimes significantly. Amongst the salient features of that development are the shifting of power relations between the Crown, Parliament and the Government in the latter's favour, and the increasing primacy of the Prime Minister. It has also offered scope for the development of a complex policy-making system, in which the actions of the *de jure powers* referred to interact with those of *de facto powers* (political parties, ideological movements, unions, groupings of all types) in an ongoing dialogue. That dialogue may sometimes turn into confrontation, but long experience in handling the system has led to positive achievements in many areas: social security, a fine balance between public and private education, and so forth. Such concerted action may arise spontaneously, or be required by law. But it has contributed, in a country where the causes of strife are myriad, to creating a climate of mutual tolerance, if not understanding, and in any event to sparing the country many of the major political problems and upsets

Belgium is a parliamentary democracy. The members of the House of Representatives and the Senate are elected every four years by all citizens entitled to vote. The photograph shows votes being counted in a polling station.

encountered elsewhere.

The most pressing problem with which Belgium's institutions are currently faced is that of the structure of the State itself, which has evolved slowly since 1830, moulded partly by the language (and to some extent, cultural) differences between north and south, and partly by economic and social developments.

The 'linguistic frontier' dividing French from Dutch has altered little over the centuries, the only change of any real note being in the capital, Brussels, which, since the early 19th century, has taken on a predominantly French hue. Today, some 80 % of the city's inhabitants have French as their first language, in a State where Dutch is the language of the majority of the population. But at the time of independence, French was the language of Belgium's ruling class, both in the north and south — a situation preserved for many decades.

Before 1830 Belgium was, moreover, in the vanguard of the first industrial revolution. For geographical reasons, however, the country's industrial base was chiefly located in Wallonia, where the only operative coal mines were to be found. Wallonia was thus the primary beneficiary of economic progress, while Flanders laboured under economic, social and cultural handicaps. Over the years, the picture gradually changed. Domestic and world economic developments led to the decline of the traditional Wallonian industries, while Flanders developed new ones at a faster pace than Wallonia. A powerful Flemish movement at the same time began to call for practical recognition of the cultural identity of Flanders. This was achieved most notably by a series of statutes governing the use of languages in education, the legal system,

the armed forces and central and local government.

This situation, coupled with Wallonia's awakening to its own plight, inspired an all-round determination to achieve greater self-government for the Flemish and Walloon populations, together with the small, German-speaking community (60,000 in all) in east Belgium. The extensive debates and controversies sparked off by this resulted in two successive revisions of the Constitution in 1970/71 and 1980. A detailed description of the highly complex system designed to achieve that independence is outside the scope of this essay. Suffice it to say that its essential features are the maintenance of existing local authority powers (provinces and municipalities, reduced by law from over 3,000 to under 600) and the creation of new, higher-tier bodies, the *Communities* and the *Regions*. These intermediate levels of government only partially superpose each other. There are now three Communities — Flemish, French and German. The two former cover the inhabitants of Flanders and Wallonia, plus the respective Flemish- or French-speaking inhabitants of Brussels. There are three Regions — Flan-

ders, Wallonia and Brussels. The German-speaking area falls under the authority of the Walloon Region. That the two types of new institution are not identical is due to the peculiar linguistic situation of the capital. Each of these institutions enjoys legislative and executive powers in areas of responsibility wholly devolved to it by central government. While the Communities have social and cultural responsibilities, those of the Regions are chiefly in the economic and regional development spheres. Central government has retained major responsibilities in all these policy areas. Conflicts of legislations between central government, the Communities and the Regions are resolved by a Court of Arbitration; conflicts of interest by a conciliation procedure.

It is not a completely federal system in the textbook sense, being at once more and less than a federation. In the autumn of 1987, Parliament and the Government therefore decided to undertake new Constitutional reforms to complete the edifice of a completely federal structure of State.

But it would be wrong to see Belgium as heading towards complete separation; the overwhelming majority of Bel-

gians have expressed the desire for the 'marriage' to continue; for they know it is in their interests to do so. They are also alive to the fact, recently confirmed by reliable studies, that beyond the singular features peculiar to each Community and Region there lies a vast body of shared values. And it is these — often more clearly perceived by outsiders than some Belgians — which form the bedrock of their union through their genuine and well-founded differences.

It must be stressed that despite the very genuine, but sometimes over-dramatized and magnified, internal problems and divisions, Belgium is today a focal point of western Europe, in which its geographical location clearly plays a large part. But it could also be said to be a microcosm in which all the problems confronting the countries of western Europe have been played out for more than a century. A turn-of-the-century French sociologist called Belgium a *land of experiences*. These factors, together with many other considerations — not least of which is the prevailing air of freedom — have doubtless played their part in the agreements which have made it the headquarters of the European Community institutions and that of the North Atlantic Treaty Organization (NATO).

Belgium, long the 'cockpit of Europe', has become the site of a more peaceful confrontation; for it is in Brussels that European unity, slowly but surely, is being forged.

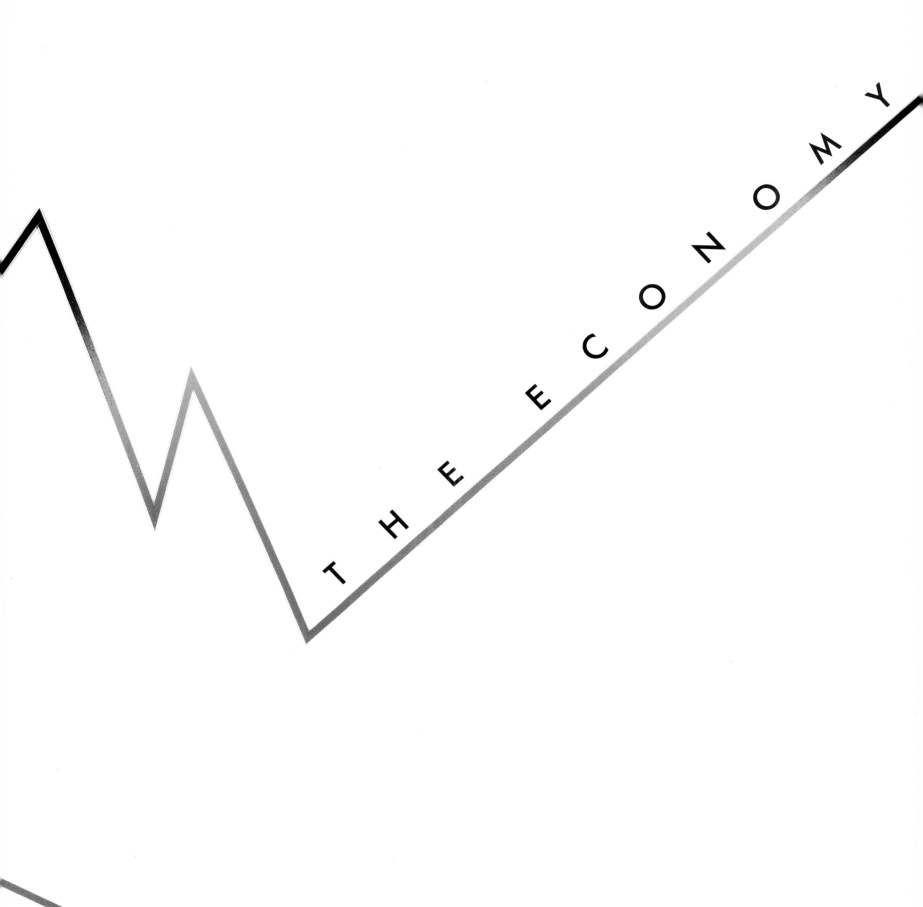

HISTORICAL DEVELOPMENT OF THE BELGIAN ECONOMY

HERMAN VAN DER WEE

THE NUCLEUS
OF PRE-INDUSTRIAL EUROPE

The provinces which today constitute the territory of Belgium have been stimulating the development of the European economy since the early days of civilisation. In the Gallo-Roman age they supplied food, clothing, footwear, weapons to the armies in England and on the Rhine border, which led to the introduction of progressive agricultural methods, dynamic textile and metal industries and a modern urbanisation system. During this period, the Belgian provinces were a model for the economic development of Northern Gaul and England. In the Middle Ages they formed the strategic economy of the Merovingian and Carolingian dynasties. Although the urban network disintegrated, as in the rest of Europe at this time, agriculture and industry remained important and formed the economic backbone of Charlemagne's empire.

The role of the Belgian provinces in the rise of commercial capitalism around the year 1000 was no less crucial. This evolution was closely connected with new progress in agriculture and the revival of the towns. The advance of agriculture was based on new techniques like the introduction of three-field rotation and the emancipation of the agricultural population through the abolition of serfdom on the great estates, two innovations which emerged mainly in the area between the Rhine and the Loire. These two big steps forward led to the intensification of agriculture and consequently a larger surplus of agricultural produce, which set the process of urbanisation in motion once again. Flanders, Brabant and the Meuse valley saw a remarkable revival or development of towns during this period.

The urban expansion of the Southern Netherlands was also stimulated by

commercial and industrial factors, like the revival of maritime trade and transcontinental overland traffic in Europe. It was also closely connected with the rise of an export-oriented urban-based textile industry. In both cases, the towns of the Southern Netherlands were the motor behind these developments. In Flanders, Brabant and the valley of the Meuse, a phenomenon was emerging which was unique in Europe at the time: the growth of specifically industrial towns, i.e. towns mainly concerned with the mass production of high-quality standardized woollen cloth, destined for export all over Europe, the Middle East and North Africa. The strength of this urban-based export industry derived from the division of labour into a great number of individual jobs and specialised tasks — in other words, a substantial increase in the productivity of labour, and from the import of the finest wools from England which led to a substantial increase in product quality. In some towns of the Meuse Valley, a similar

metallurgical export industry developed.

The towns of the Southern Netherlands continued to forge ahead, and their merchant-adventurers organised not only a flourishing maritime trade with England but also the export of their goods all over Europe. This stimulated transcontinental overland traffic and thereby promoted the growth of towns throughout Europe. This also led to fruitful contacts with the towns of Northern and Central Italy, who could expand their trade with the Middle East and North Africa substantially through the export of woollen cloth from the Southern Netherlands, and consolidate their dominant position in the transit trade of the Mediterranean and the Black Sea area. The Italian expansion also penetrated northwards, and merchants from Italy were to become the most important purchasers of woollen cloth from the South Netherlands at the annual fair in Champagne. In due course they also set up direct shipping

links between their home ports in Italy and Bruges-Antwerp, the ports serving the economic growth centre of Northwest Europe.

The high degree of division of labour in the urban export industries meant that semi-skilled workers could be employed on a large scale. Moreover, the technology required in these industries was very primitive, and these two factors made urban industry extremely vulnerable. A successful export product from one town could easily be copied by another, and this is exactly what happened. If the export industry of a certain town expanded too quickly, the cost of living also rose in that town, and claims for higher wages became more insistent. Rising production costs were then an invitation for smaller centres in the region with lower production costs to launch cheaper imitations on the market.

The production of woollen cloth in smaller centres led to a very rapid increase in the number of industrial

During the Middle Ages, Ypres was one of the most powerful towns of Flanders. The Cloth Halls were destroyed in the First World War, and painstakingly rebuilt afterwards.

towns in the Southern Netherlands. Simple imitations were followed by more inventive variations, so that a highly diverse textile industry was gradually built up in the region. Textiles from the Southern Netherlands thus became a dominant industrial product throughout Europe and the Middle East in the 13th and 14th centuries.

The towns threatened by these cheaper imitations tried to adapt to the new situation. They concentrated on the production of the finest and most expensive cloths, a field in which they had a comparative advantage, and where higher wage costs were less of a handicap. Then came the idea of 'New draperies' and 'Light draperies' to replace the 'Old draperies' ('New draperies': traditional heavy cloth, woven with wool of lesser quality; 'Light draperies': cloth of good quality but of lesser weight, according to changes in taste and fashion). Finally, they introduced new industries and services, and creativity became the key to a structural transformation. In the textile sector, a whole series of specialist industries for luxury goods emerged, based on highly-skilled labour, artistic inventiveness and a feeling for fashionable discrimination in taste: tapestry weaving, embroidery, lace-making and the clothing industry. The latter branched out into more specialised activities like millinery, hosiery, glove-making, shoe-making and furriery, to name a few. In some towns, textile finishing expanded into a thriving separate branch of industry, processing cloth from England and other countries as well as local textiles. Outside the textile sector, many other luxury industries also began to flourish around this time.

In the art sector painting, and the Flemish Primitives in particular, were the spearhead of this expansion which grew to include miniature painting,

gold and silverwork, altarpieces, furniture-making, musical instrument making and diamond work. Other flourishing sectors included: the manufacture of luxury boxes, clockmaking, bellfounding, the arms industry, brasswork and later bookprinting etc. In the services sector, new and more sophisticated forms of education, music and entertainment emerged: the schools of polyphonic music were the most innovative in this field. Finally, a financial services sector evolved in Bruges, Mechelen, Antwerp and Liège: deposit and giro banks were set up, consumer credit increased explosively, bills of exchange were widely used, which of course also led to the introduction of arbitrage on the international exchange market.

The large towns, which were the first to be hit by imitation and outside competition, were also the first to adapt structurally to the new situation. Gradually, industry in the smaller centres was also restructured: weaving and the clothing trade, for instance, expanded fast in the smaller towns. The rapid expansion of corporatism during this period resulted in the organization of highly-skilled workers into specialised trades, thereby guaranteeing an effective quality control on new products. In this way, corporatism institutionalised the structural transformation of urban industry in the Southern Netherlands. The luxury products produced in these towns soon found a market abroad. However, they were only exported on a limited scale in the 14th and 15th centuries because the development of a prosperous, flourishing economy in the Low Countries themselves under the Dukes of Burgundy generated ample demand for these new products locally. This changed dramatically in the course of the 16th century. The general increase in prosperity

throughout the rest of Europe stimulated a demand for luxury goods which could only be met in the short term by the urban industry of Italy and the Southern Netherlands. As a result, these luxury sectors developed into powerful export industries in the 16th century, dominating together with Italy the whole of the European market and even penetrating America via Spain. The specialised services also played an active role in export: schools in the towns opened their doors to a stream of pupils from abroad, coming to be trained as bookkeepers, merchants or musicians. The export boom in the luxury industries multiplied the number of highly-skilled workers in the towns, and raised the level of their skills. This made it possible to set up new industries to replace imports of luxury goods from Italy and the Middle East. Workshops were established for glassblowing and the manufacture of mirrors and majolica ware, and of course the silk industry was established. The latter was by far the most important: before the century was out, it had developed from an import-subsitution industry into a fully-fledged, dynamic export industry in its own right, employing thousands of workers.

But the urban luxury industries and specialised services were not the only sectors which turned to export in the 16th century: rural industry was also successful in this respect. Rural industry came into being at the end of the Middle Ages, when low prices for agricultural produce prompted farmers to supplement their income by industrial labour. During this period, goods manufactured in this way were only sold locally or to neighbouring regions, but during the course of the century, rural industry developed into a significant export sector. Light-weight woollen and linen cloths woven in rural Flan-

ders found a fast-growing market in Italy, the Levant and the New World. Woollen cloth, linens and tick from rural Brabant were exported to Central Europe and Spain. Metalware, especially nails and simple weapons manufactured by Walloon farmers in the winter months, also found its way abroad. These exports were all standardized products which could be mass-produced and which were therefore suitable for production methods based on the principle of division of labour. In this way, use could be made of the cheap, semi-skilled labour available in rural areas where unemployment would otherwise have been rife.

The spectacular growth of the Southern Netherlands exports during the 16th century collapsed at the end of the century with the Revolt of the Netherlands against Spain. However, the first half of the 17th century saw a strong recovery in this respect. The export of paintings, tapestries, furniture and printed matter flourished as never before. Rubens, van Dijck, Jordaens and Teniers enjoyed world-wide fame, as did the printer/publisher Plantijn-Moretus and the great tapestry weavers of Brussels and Antwerp. During the same period, exports of lacework and silk also reached a peak. Yet more export sectors emerged, for products like organs, harpsichords and carillons. Meanwhile, exports of Flemish furnishing textiles (curtains, upholstering fabrics, bedspreads, linen etc.) also followed a steady upward trend. Ribbon-weaving became a leading sector in the clothing industry.

The export boom of the Southern Netherlands industries during the 16th and 17th centuries would not have been possible without the support of a strong commercial and financial infrastructure. Bruges, which had been the leading trade centre of Northwest

Europe in the late Middle Ages, could not maintain its powerful position. In the 17th century it was overtaken by Antwerp, which rose to the status of the greatest trade metropolis in the West. The Port of Antwerp became one of the most important ports in the world at that time, perhaps even the most important of all. The Antwerp annual fair evolved into the largest permanent staple market in the world. English woollen cloth, spices from the East, copper from Southern Germany, silver from America and many other goods all passed through this staple market on their way to destinations all over the world. The export of goods produced by the urban and rural industries of the Southern Netherlands was organized from this staple market. And the import of a wide variety of raw materials, foodstuffs and foreign specialities into the Netherlands also went through the Antwerp market.

Not only was Antwerp the major trade centre of the world in the 16th century, it also developed into the leading money and capital market. Bruges had already performed this role for Northwest Europe at the end of the Middle Ages. From about 1520 onwards, Antwerp took over the financial functions of Bruges and was for a time the leading financial centre of the world. As early as 1531, the first Exchange in Europe was opened in Antwerp. Soon after, new financial techniques were introduced in Antwerp which opened the way to our modern monetary and banking systems. For instance, it was in Antwerp that the transferability of commercial papers was reinforced by the introduction of the principle of negotiability by means of the assignment and endorsement formula. From this time on, the circulation of commercial papers from hand to hand increased sharply, preparing the way for the

breakthrough of the modern bank note. Antwerp also introduced the technique of discounting bonds and bills of exchange, which was a big step in the direction of our modern discount houses. The maritime insurance world of Antwerp and its commercial law were models for ports and markets throughout Northwest Europe. Finally, a capital market for government securities was built up in Antwerp, and this was to become the cornerstone of modern public finance.

The ambitious world policies of the Hapsburg monarchy and the Eighty Years' War ruined the financial hegemony of Antwerp. The money and capital market of Antwerp became first an appendage of the exchange markets of Genoa and later a simple satellite of Amsterdam. Trade and industry in the Southern Netherlands were also in decline during this period. Immediately after the Spanish armies had reconquered the Southern Netherlands at the end of the 16th century, tens of thousands of specialised craftsmen, entrepreneurs, merchants and bankers had already fled, mainly to the Northern Netherlands but also to Germany, England, France, and even to the New World. This wave of emigration carried out the industrial, commercial and financial know-how of the Southern Netherlands to the rest of Europe, where it sowed

the seeds of a successful import-substitution industry in those lands. Nevertheless, the export industry of the Southern Netherlands enjoyed a temporary revival in the first half of the 17th century. However, this was followed by a definitive decline which was caused by the rise of mercantilism all over Europe, coupled with the strengthening of the European national states. The European governments of the time followed a systematic policy of protectionism and import-substitution, and attracted workers from abroad with the promise of high wages. Emigration was once again the order of the day in the Southern Netherlands.

However, the decline of the specialised export industry in the towns of the Southern Netherlands did not destroy the creativity of the region. The focus shifted from the towns to the rural areas, to agriculture and rural industry. During the expansion of the 16th century, there had been an urban population explosion. This increased imports of grain and livestock for consumption, and also stimulated the introduction of more intensive farming methods in the region. As a result of this, a highly progressive agricultural economy evolved in Flanders and Brabant, and agriculture in the Northern Netherlands benefited greatly from methods developed in the South. England, too,

followed the example of Flanders and Brabant, adopting their intensive farming techniques which in the course of the 17th Century generated the Agricultural Revolution in England. This paved the way for the Industrial Revolution of the 18th century, and the urbanisation which went with it.

Linen weaving in rural Flanders and the iron and coal industries of rural Wallonia were a second factor in the rural creativity of the 17th and 18th centuries. This combination of agricultural and industrial activities optimized production costs and laid the foundations for a powerful expansion of linen, nail and coal exports. In Wallonia, this expansion prepared the way for the rise of modern heavy industry, while in Flanders it promoted trade in Ghent, thereby also favouring the development of a mechanised cotton industry.

A PIONEER IN THE INDUSTRIALISATION OF EUROPE

To understand the specific nature of the Industrial Revolution in Belgium, both technological and institutional determining factors have to be taken into account. In addition to the general characteristics of the Industrial Revolution everywhere, there are also specific factors which are unique to Belgium, especially in the context of

Manor-farm in Roly (in the province of Namur).

Belgium's development between 1770 and 1847.

The early industrialisation of the region (Belgium was the first country in the world to adopt the British industrialisation model successfully) cannot be attributed solely to the availability of coal and iron ore in Wallonia, however strategically opportune they were for Belgium's industrialisation at this period. A multitude of organizational and institutional factors played an equally decisive role. Progress in agriculture over the 18th century led to a larger surplus of agricultural produce which was first used for export and later also to meet the requirements of further demographic growth. During the Austrian period, the general infrastructure was also improved considerably. A good, modern transport network was established at this time. Both in the towns and in the country, cottage industry had mushroomed. It depended on home-based workers under the leadership of dynamic merchant-entrepreneurs who applied the well-known 'putting out' system. This tapped a vast pool of industrial labour available to urban entrepreneurs with daring and talent.

The decisive industrial breakthrough in Belgium came in the first half of the 19th century, when industry crystallized around five main growth poles: Liège-Verviers, Mons-Charleroi, Ghent, Brussels and Antwerp. In the area around Liège and Verviers, the new development model was put into practice in the wool industry and above all in the coal and iron sectors. Hainault also saw the birth of a modern metallurgical and coal industry, later joined by a flourishing glass industry. Ghent became the centre of the cotton industry. At the same time, rural Flanders wasted its industrial potential by clinging stubbornly and exclusively to the tradition-al but now obsolescent flax and linen sector, soon to be overtaken by other rising industries. In Brussels, a modern tertiary sector evolved under the leadership of the financial middle class, which had close links with the government. And lastly, the economic blossoming of Antwerp was based mainly on its port activities: trade with the colonies, insurance, transit trade and the processing industry.

The strength of the Belgian Industrial Revolution lay above all in the mechanisation of the heavy industry in Wallonia. Liège and Hainault were indisputably the most dynamic regions in the country. Despite the swift mechanisation of the textile industry in Belgium, the sector failed to attain the spearhead position it enjoyed in Britain. This was due primarily to the political problems of the first half of the 19th century which repeatedly suspended foreign export and made a harmonious evolution of the sector impossible. An additional handicap for Belgium was of course the fact that Britain was technically far in advance in the textile sector.

The industrial production of foodstuffs played no part whatsoever in the first phase of industrialisation, and the same is true of consumer durables. This can be largely explained by the modest scale of the national market. The extremely low level of wages was another significant factor here: the high population density, which was a legacy from the move to the towns in the late Middle Ages, and the concentration of labour in an obsolescent rural industry generated a substantial labour surplus in the transition to modern industrial methods. Wages therefore remained around subsistence level. Because basic industry was accounting for a growing proportion of industrial activity during the industrialisation process, the relative surplus of labour continued to increase: industrialisation indeed was a capital-intensive rather than labour-intensive operation.

The unequal distribution of income in Belgium held back the development of a domestic market for consumer goods, and also prevented a more equal distribution of wealth. If these two effects were also unfavourable from a social point of view, the latter did present some positive aspects in the context of economic development: the concentration of wealth in Belgium allowed a new spearhead sector to emerge in the form of commercial banking. The establishment of this financial sector in Brussels, which was both fortunate and skilful enough to take advantage of the industrial expansion in Wallonia, exerted a dynamic influence on the course of the Belgian Industrial Revolution.

The Belgian industrialisation process in the 19th century was therefore advancing intermittently on two fronts: that of technology on the one hand, and organization on the other. Technological progress was first based on the imitation of English techniques, but later an autonomous Belgian evolution gathered momentum. There was a growing desire to catch up with or even overtake England in the technological field. During the initial phase, modern British technology had to be adapted to the geographical, artisanal and institutional circumstances in Belgium, which required a creative approach. This creativity led to the development of new technical know-how and autonomous innovations which could be exported to the rest of Europe.

Resounding technological successes were notched up by companies in the Belgian mining industry. The Letoret pump, the Lessines ventilator, the Warocquière lift and the Coppée family's many patents were all great innovations which were introduced in all the mining areas of continental Europe. The Mining School of Mons in Hainault provided top-grade training, and many engineering graduates came from abroad to study there, especially from France. The coal basins of the Loire and Northern France, which were developed in the second half of the 19th century, leaned heavily on Belgian technology. The same phenomenon occurred with the industrialisation of the German Ruhr. Belgian influence was even stronger in Luxembourg and Lorraine: the great iron and steel companies of Belgium obtained mining concessions for iron ore and built the most advanced type of blast furnaces there.

Belgian technology in the manufacture of zinc was also on a world level. In 1805, Jacques-Daniel Dony in Liège had developed a new and efficient method for the reduction of zinc ore from the rich mining area of Moresnet. This invention led to the establishment of the 'Société de la Vieille Montagne' which went on to modernise Belgian zinc production as a whole. Within a short space of time, companies were also set up abroad to exploit the new technology generated in Liège. Similar successes were achieved in the Belgian glass and wool industries. The glass industry in Hainault won world fame on the basis of its autonomously developed technology, and it soon reached a position where it could export 85 % of its massive production of glass. In the wool sector it was the invention of the Levrathan wool washing machine in 1863 which promoted the Verviers region to the status of a world export centre for wool.

Although the stream of technological innovations was of the utmost importance for the success of Belgian industrialisation, the progress made in the field of industrial and above all financial

One upon a time, Belgian coal generated wealth and prosperity and huge industrial development. Today, many mines lie derelict. A museum of industrial archeology has been set up in the lift shaft 'Belle Fleur' of the long-closed mine in Bois du Luc.

organization was no less essential. The birth of mixed banking was of paramount importance, together with the modern holding company formula. Both were specifically Belgian inventions, and both were to exert a powerful and stimulating influence on the industrialisation process in Belgium and the whole world.

In 1822 King William I founded the 'Société Générale des Pays-Bas pour favoriser l'industrie nationale', thereafter called simply the 'Société Générale'. Although this company was conceived as a development bank, that was not how it worked in practice. A few long-term credits were granted to a limited number of shipping canal companies and rising large-scale enterprises like Cockerill, but the rest of the Société Générale's activities concentrated on short-term actions and the management of State finances. However, in the course of the economic crisis which followed the Belgian Independence in 1830, a series of participations in the coal industry and local metallurgical companies in the Borinage came into the possession of the Société Générale, as a result of the reorganization of short-term credits. After several years' hesitation, the directors of the Société Générale began to realise the importance of an industrial portfolio. They therefore made a resolute decision to transform Hainault into a modern industrial region, aiming at the attractive potential market in France. The French economy had an urgent need for heavy industry products, and lacked a modern production structure of its own in this sector. France preferred to depend on Belgium rather than Britain for imports, because it had nothing to fear politically from Belgium. Moreover, Belgian industry had the strong geographical advantage of being close to Lorraine.

The new strategy of the Société Générale, oriented towards long-term participations in modern industry, was also well-founded from a political point of view. Immediately after the Independence of Belgium in 1830, the Société Générale was suspected of Orangeist sympathies. It was therefore not at all certain that it would be permitted to carry on managing the State finances for the Belgian government. Then a competitor was set up by the Belgian Liberals in 1835: the 'Banque de Belgique'. Moreover, the enlightened despotism of William I had given way to a liberal ideology in which the task of the State was drastically reduced. Under such circumstances, no substantial demand for credit could be expected from the State. On the other hand, there were very attractive long-term investment opportunities in industry, especially in the basic sectors. The modernisation of heavy industry and the transport revolution triggered a gigantic demand for capital which could not possibly be met by autofinancing. The Société Générale and the Banque de Belgique were able and flexible enough to take advantage of this huge demand for investment, and this sowed the seeds of an intense rivalry between the two institutions, with a very positive spin-off for the modernisation of heavy industry.

By setting up branch offices, the two banks achieved both vertical and horizontal integration with the companies they controlled: a formula which was a forerunner of the holding structure of today. However, it also contained a series of weaknesses which were among the main factors leading up to the serious financial crisis of 1848. The system was refined and strengthened by the creation of the National Bank of Belgium in 1850. This institutional reform proved to be an enormous success: it guaranteed a high degree of sta-

bility in the Belgian financial system. In this climate of greater stability, the mixed banking formula could be used to create a mini capital market within each financial group, thus providing a clearer view of the group finances as a whole. The long-term investment strategies could be optimized within these mini-capital markets, while the central bank provided for the availability of liquid assets.

The Belgian mixed banks turned their considerable innovative powers of organization to setting up a network of modern companies in Belgium and abroad. They played a leading role in building national and local railway lines in Belgium, Europe and all over the world. At the same time they created a market for Belgian heavy industry, and promoted the establishment of new manufacturing industries in Belgium, particularly for the manufacture of rolling stock. They also introduced modern firms in the heavy industry sector abroad. The expansion of the industrial market to cover the whole of Europe and later the whole world was completed on the organizational level by the integration of the Port of Antwerp into the Belgian banking complex.

Round the turn of the century, about 90 % of the fifty largest non-financial companies in Belgium belonged to heavy industry and the traditional transport sector: proof of the enormous expansion thrust generated by the mixed banking world in Belgium. Around this same time, the system was consolidated and Belgium was overtaken in the international race of the technological revolution. The innovations of the second half of the 19th century which had prepared the way for the development of new industrial spearhead sectors and which would exert such a dynamic influence on the industrialization process in Germany and America, now

failed to be assimilated completely in the investment strategy of the Belgian banking world. The effectiveness of the mixed banks formula and the investment strategy implemented was maintained in the established sectors. But it became increasingly clear that the close link between the Belgian financial world and traditional industry was becoming more and more of a handicap to the revival and diversification of the economy.

During the 19th century, the mixed banks of Brussels had shown no interest in the mechanization of the textile industry in Flanders, where low wages also held back the pace of mechanization. It was above all the smaller family firms in Flanders which gradually got the modernization process underway. The fact that the new firms were preponderantly family firms tended to increase the fragmentation of the industrial structure, but it also increased the adaptability and flexibility of investment strategy.

THE DIFFICULT INTERWAR PERIOD

The First World War caused a sudden and dangerous break in the development of the Belgian economy. The German victory brought great devastation and misery, and the fighting on the IJzer cost many lives. Industrial production collapsed. The Germans even dismantled a large part of the industry. After the war, new problems emerged. The inflation which had raised its head during the war could not be brought under control after the war. This put heavy pressure on the real incomes of the wage-earners, because wage increases trailed along far behind rising prices. Fortunately, this was counterbalanced to a certain extent by the fact that social services and welfare provisions were established by law and organized efficiently for the first time during and immediately after the war.

Albert-Edouard Janssen, as Minister of Finance, tried to achieve currency reform between 1925-26 on the basis of a

Belgium was one of the first industrial states of continental Europe. Over the last few years there has been a new revival of Belgian industry, marked by the reconstruction or closure of obsolescent enterprises.

limited devaluation of the Belgian franc. But the rate chosen was too high, the recovery of the budget balance too elementary and incomplete, and the lack of confidence and cooperation from the Belgian banks was too great. Janssen failed. Panic then broke out and continued to reign until Emile Francqui arrived on the scene and restored the balance of the budget by drastic measures, stabilising the franc at a level which undervalued the Belgian currency abysmally with respect to the rest of the world.

Francqui's currency reform had an immediate and very favourable effect on Belgian industry. The stabilization restored confidence in the country. At the same time, the undervaluation of the franc promoted export. A golden era dawned for entrepreneurs, and the workers also profited from the increase in production because it brought a substantial increase in employment. But the workers had a price to pay: in spite of the improved economic situation, the wage level had dropped in real terms. On the other hand, the revival of Belgian industry had a positive effect on profit margins and stimulated companies to invest and expand. The mixed banks were very active in this field. They showed a clear preference for investments in the old sectors of industry which entailed fewer risks, and turned their backs on investments in new sectors. The mixed banks of Brussels increased their participations in heavy industry in Belgium and abroad, e.g. in the Balkans. They also invested more and more, and with increasing enthusiasm, in the development of mining in the Belgian Congo. There they also found a wide field for investment on a grand scale in the transport sector. And finally they also undertook the further rationalization of the companies they patronized, by means of financial oper-

ations like mergers, take-overs, vertical and horizontal integration.

During the Twenties, a specifically Flemish type of mixed banking developed, based on the savings of the labourers, agricultural workers and urban middle classes. Flemish mixed banks invested in many young firms, especially in the agricultural and textile sectors in Flanders. Gradually they began to invest in other branches of industry in Belgium, and in the years of feverish speculation from 1926 onwards, they also invested heavily abroad.

The flourishing Belgian industry of the Twenties was seriously undermined by the great world crisis of the next decade. The collapse of world trade was an immediate threat to Belgium's small open economy, which depended to a large extent on export.

The situation deteriorated from the moment the British and American governments withdrew from the gold standard at the beginning of the Thirties. A few European countries, including Belgium, reacted against the floating exchange rates of the pound and the dollar by setting up the Gold Bloc which remained faithful to the gold standard and the system of stable exchange rates. The value of the Belgian franc rose sharply against the sterling and dollar zones, and soon found itself in an overvalued position. To try and prevent a further collapse of export, the government introduced a deflationary policy. The lower prices which resulted from the world crisis and the Belgian deflation policy raised the real wage level, but this offered little comfort for the ever-swelling ranks of the unemployed.

The coupling of wages to the declining retail price index soon led to the reduction of the nominal income of those who managed to find work. Reactions

followed, which persuaded the government to take measures to partially disconnect wages from the retail price index again, and to shift the focus of the deflation policy to the monetary sector and control of budget deficits. The banks, which were badly hit by dwindling deposits and the general decline of trade, came up against liquidity problems. The government granted support for special credit loans, but this was strictly limited by the restrictions of the deflation policy in force.

The Flemish banks, which had pursued a dynamic investment strategy in the Twenties, were in the most vulnerable position in the growing liquidity crisis. Some of them crashed in the course of 1934 and others faced serious financial difficulties. Although the banks in Brussels had been more cautious in their investments, they too were caught up in the crisis. They had used their short-term deposits to extend cash credits and advances to the companies in which they had a participation. These cash credits were largely frozen as a result of the unfavourable export climate, and had therefore lost their liquidity. The panic which broke out as a reaction to the wave of bankruptcies in the financial sector increased the pressure on deposits. The bank crisis now took on a more general character and began to threaten the economic stability of the whole country.

A first attempt to get the situation back on a sound basis was undertaken in 1934, and consisted of splitting the mixed banks into holding companies. and deposit banks. Gustaaf Sap, the Finance Minister who devised this measure, believed that this would restore confidence in banking and prevent a general rush to withdraw deposits, thereby averting the danger of a general bank crisis. At the same time, Sap hoped, with the support of the National

Bank, that the Belgian franc could be maintained at its 1926 exchange rate.

Gradually the principle of holding on to the 1926 par value became the subject of more and more fierce argument. The sharp fall of the pound sterling increased the negative effect of the world crisis on Belgian exports. The Louvain school of economists, under the leadership of Léon-Henri Dupriez, propagated the idea that the government could no longer avoid devaluing the Belgian franc. Finally, Van Zeeland's government (25 March 1935 - 26 May 1936) did in fact devalue the Belgian franc by 28 %. The tension then relaxed in the bank crisis, and in other sectors signs of recovery were soon to be seen. For the workers, this was a signal to take action to demand a share in the new rise in the national income. This action led to the organization of the first National Labour Conference on 17 June 1936. Important improvements were won for wage-earners and salaried employees, as well as substantial improvements in secondary conditions of employment, such as the 40-hour week for some sectors, and paid holidays.

The crisis in Belgium had consolidated the general consensus that the political institutions of the country and the economic ideology, which was still largely dominated by the liberal tradition of 'laissez-faire', was no longer in tune with the times. The crisis had demonstrated clearly that a completely free market economy was not capable of guaranteeing monetary stability, economic growth and full employment. Various plans were elaborated, each aiming at a thorough reform of the existing structure of state. The Christian democrats put the emphasis on cooperation between the social partners, but wanted to transfer the leadership of this cooperation to the state. The Socialists went further in their proposals for the expansion of state control. By Christmas 1933 they had already presented an anti-crisis programme in the form of the Labour Plan, which was to go down in history as the De Man Plan, after Hendrik De Man, the inspiration behind the plan and a tireless fighter for the economic reform. The De Man Plan set out a number of concrete measures to combat the economic depression and also proposed a number of structural panies. These proposals remained the basis of the bill drawn up by the Liberal Minister of Finance Max-Léo Gérard, but the concept of state control was radically modified. Control was seen more as a form of flexible cooperation between the government and private banking. Moreover, the control system was to be limited mainly to the deposit banks.

credit supplies in the country had become inadequate. New instruments were required to expand the control system. The law of 1935 establishing the Bank Commission was the first step in this process of renewal.

The monetary and financial reforms of the Thirties laid the foundations of the revival of Belgian industry and Belgian export. They also laid the foundations

The Brussels Stock Exchange in the turbulent Thirties.

reforms. Further, it called for the establishment of a national organization for economic recovery (OREC), through which technocrats with ministerial powers would lead the economy.

The Royal Decree of 9 July 1935 elaborated a structural reform of the Belgian banking sector by splitting of the mixed banks in deposit banks and portfolio companies as announced in 1934. OREC's original proposals were oriented towards stricter state control of private banks, including holding com-

Be this as it may, state control of the financial sector had become a fact of life. This was a radical turnabout in the economic history of Belgium and the end of the myth that the National Bank alone had the function of creating money, and that it could control the whole credit sector through its discount policy. Since the beginning of the century, private banks had built up such a dominant role in the field of generating money and offering credit facilities that the traditional supervision by the National Bank of the money and

for the restructuring of the Belgian economy and the creation of new manufacturing sectors. At the same time, the crisis of the Thirties led to a reform of social relations in Belgium: opposition gave way to discussion and cooperation. The Second World War disturbed this evolution for a time, but thereafter the way was open to a new era of successful expansion and increasing prosperity.

ECONOMIC DEVELOPMENT AFTER WORLD WAR II

PHILIPPE BODSON

1945-85 IN A NUTSHELL

Immediately after the war

The effect of the Second World War on Belgian industry was less dramatic than that of the First World War, when production broke down completely. This was caused by the lack of raw materials, the people's refusal to work for the enemy, the lower productivity of a workforce suffering from malnutrition, and above all by the requisitioning and dismantling of the factories.

In 1917 and 1918, industrial output dropped to 30 % of the 1913 level, and it was five years before output again reached this level, in 1923.

During the Second World War, fewer factories were destroyed or dismantled, and industrial output dropped only by 35 % in 1942 and 1943 as compared with the pre-war level. This dropped further to 65 % in 1944, mainly as a result of the almost complete paralysation of transport caused by the military operations.

Steelworkers enjoy much better working conditions today than in the 19th century.

Consequently, production could get underway again much more quickly after the Second World War, and by 1947, just two years later, industrial output had again reached the pre-war level. The port of Antwerp was the only port among its competitors to have come through the war more or less intact, and was used on a large scale by Allied troops, and this was to facilitate the recovery of Belgium and generate substantial foreign currency earnings.

The fifties

On the international scene, these years are characterised by more or less successful attempts at European cooperation. In 1948, the three Benelux countries signed the Benelux Customs Union, thereby setting up the first free trade area. The Intra-European Pay-

ments Agreement inspired by the Marshall Plan made intra-European payments easier to effect and was in fact the first step towards the multilateralisation of trade in Europe. The Treaty of Paris (1951) established the European Coal and Steel Community (ECSC), which opened up European frontiers for these two primary industrial products. After the failure of the European Defence Community, the Treaty of Rome, signed in 1957, set up the European Economic Community, which first concentrated its efforts on gradually phasing out internal customs barriers and introducing a common external customs tariff.

Before these efforts towards economic cooperation began to bear fruit, the economic climate in Belgium was still characterised by the protectionism which was built up in the period between the two world wars, and the fragmentation of its markets.

Consequently, the traditional structure of Belgian industry, which was based on the manufacture of semi-finished goods, hardly changed during this decade, especially with a substantial demand for these products from a Europe (and indeed a world) busy reconstructing.

The most characteristic example of this development phase can be seen in the metallurgical industry, where primary products (steel and nonferrous metals) forged ahead while growth in the processing sector merely kept time with the GNP.

The primary sector of this industry saw its share in GNP grow from 2 % to 3.5 % between 1950 and 1960, while the processing sector stagnated around 8 %.

A similar evolution could be observed in the chemical industry, where the

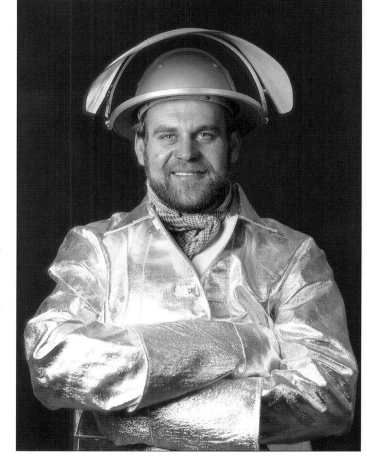

heavy chemical sector grew faster than fine chemicals, and in the textile industry, where the manufacture of semi-finished goods (yarns) grew faster than the weaving sector.

An analysis of industrial investment during this period shows more defensive investments than investments for expansion. Faced with gradually increasing competition, entrepreneurs invested to lower the cost price, raise productivity and improve quality. The level of private enterprise investment in the manufacture of new products was lagging behind that of our neighbours. Moreover, during the same period, the booming Congolese economy was draining both risk capital and enterprising compatriots out of the country.

The golden sixties

This decade saw a fast and continuous expansion which was to last right up to 1974.

The Belgian economy was swept along on the tide of world economic expansion during this period, and its central location in Europe enabled it to profit richly from the new opportunities offered by the Common Market. Belgium reached its peak performance during these fourteen years. The new foreign subsidiaries opened in Belgium during this period indicated that their contribution to the economy was then at its height, even without taking account of growth through the foreign companies established in our country at an earlier date.

The average annual growth of the GNP rose to 5 %, as against 2.9 % in the fifties.

This time, the boom industries were the metal processing sector and the chemical industry, which were the main beneficiaries of the spate of foreign investment attracted by Belgium's strategic position at the centre of the EEC, the workforce available — especially in the north — and the generous welcome of the Belgian Government.

These foreign companies and the efforts of some Belgian firms led to greater diversification and a better industrial structure, which, however, still proved to be inadequate in the crisis years.

The economic crisis (1975-81)

The inflationary pressures of the last years of the previous period were a clear sign that world economy was about to go into steep decline.

The first oil price shock lit the fuse and the crisis exploded. With its wide open economy, Belgium was bound to be shaken to its foundations. Moreover, a failure to adapt policies accordingly during the early years of the crisis made the effects of the crisis even more disastrous in Belgium.

The decline in exchange terms as a result of rising energy costs and higher prices for certain raw materials, should have been counterbalanced by austerity measures on the domestic front. But that did not happen. The maintenance of a system of full and automatic wage indexation, additional pay benefits granted by employers at the end of the period of prosperity, and the higher social security contributions imposed by the government, now combined to produce a real explosion of wage costs. The economic sectors most exposed to international competition were the first

to see their competitive position decline sharply. More and more closures and restructuring operations in private enterprise caused the level of employment to drop alarmingly. The Government tried to turn the tide by granting massive subsidies to certain sectors and to many individual companies.

Efforts to combat unemployment entailed extra expenditure, but tax revenues were no longer growing so fast as a result of the decline in business activity. Raising taxes substantially failed to bridge this gap. The result was a growing budget deficit which reached a record level of 13.4 % of the GNP in 1981. Added to this, the artificial maintenance of domestic purchasing power pushed the current balance of payments into the red, leading in 1981 to a deficit of 200,000 million BF or 5.5 % of the GNP.

A difficult recovery

A change of policy came in 1982. In the first place, the emphasis was on restoring competitiveness and strengthening the financial structure of business and industrial interprises. This aimed to promote the growth of export, which would bring more employment opportunities and also take some of the pressure off the state finances.

This policy did have some effect, but its success was limited at first, mainly as a result of the unfavourable international situation. Further decline was at least halted. However, state finances failed to improve, as a result of the increasing pressure of interest payments on the national debt, and in spite of the sharp increase in fiscal revenues.

From 1985 onwards, the emphasis shifted to reducing government spending radically as a means of getting the national finances back on a sound footing. This has yielded tangible re-

sults, although the budgetary situation in Belgium is still much less healthy than in most other European countries. Private enterprise investments have shown an upward trend since 1984, and this is one of the factors which has helped to slow down the growth of unemployment, which, however, still remains a cause for concern.

PRODUCTION AND EXPORT STRUCTURE

The structure of production and export has changed quite radically over the last forty years. In the first place, the relative importance of agriculture in Belgium fell back dramatically. Industry, too, was hit hard from 1974 on, after an initial period of growth which, however, did not significantly increase its share in the GNP. Each sector of industry has its own tale to tell. The chemical, food and metal processing industries, for instance, were more re-

silient, while the textile sector and the primary metallurgical industry faced greater problems. The picture in the extractive industries mirrored the crisis dominating the coal industry from 1957 onwards, while electricity and gas continued to thrive as a result.

The service sector progressed relatively fast, gathering even greater momentum after 1974 and pointing to Belgium's future as a services-based economy. The growth in the tertiary sector is primarily in the field of finance, the medical professions and public services.

Like all small industrial countries, Belgium is wide open to foreign trade. This growing openness is one of the most characteristic phenomena of the last decades. Export of goods and services, expressed as a percentage of the total available (GNP + imports) grew from 23 % in 1953 to 26 % in 1960 and 46 % in 1985. The import figures are almost identical. There are a variety of

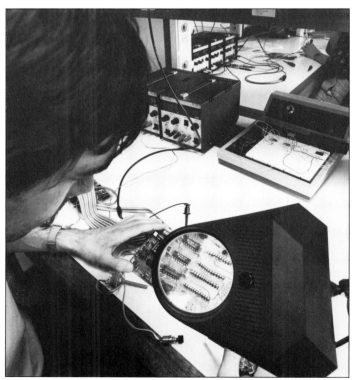

The economic crisis which began in the Seventies swept over Belgium too. New opportunities are created for the young unemployed through retraining schemes set up by the state Employment Department.

factors explaining this exceptionally swift growth of our economy's dependence on the rest of the world. The general development of international trade is one of them, and the opening up of frontiers, particularly through the establishment of the Common Market, Belgium's favourable geographical position within the EEC, the presence in our country of subsidiaries of multinationals in processing and export activities (such as automobile assembly), and more recently, the crisis itself, which has led to more international restructuring and specialisation.

The various sectors of industry have profited in varying degrees from these market opportunities.

The most marked progress is to be found among the chemical products, which have proportionally doubled their share in Belgian exports as a whole. There was also a marked improvement in the metal processing sector, at least between 1959-70. However, the primary metallurgical industry, both steel and nonferrous metals, has declined in relation to other sectors, especially since 1974. Textile and clothing exports have also declined sharply, but this trend appears to have levelled out over the last five years.

The relative importance of the services sector in our foreign trade relations has expanded enormously: from less than 25 % in 1970 to about 40 % today.

The Belgium-Luxembourg Economic Union is among the leaders in the international field for tertiary sector foreign trade. A study carried out by the British Invisible Exports Council showed that in 1983, the volume of invisible exports from the BLEU was only surpassed by the USA, UK, France and Japan, and that they were number eight in the ranking according to net surplus on the balance of payments for the services

sector, after the above-mentioned four countries plus Switzerland, Austria and Singapore. Considering the size of its economy as a whole, this was a remarkable achievement. In the world league table of exporting countries, the BLEU ranks about tenth, and for income from invisible exports it ranks even higher.

The geographical orientation of trade has characteristically focused on the EEC market, which has absorbed about 70 % of our exports for many years.

Within the ECC, our main customers are the Federal Republic of Germany and France. The proportion of exports to the Netherlands is declining, although this is partly because the preferentiality we used to enjoy in this market through the Benelux agreements has gradually disappeared with the development of the EEC.

The massive reorientation of our sales towards the EEC has entailed a relative decline of export to other countries, particularly the USA and Latin America. The developing countries account for about 10 % of our sales.

EMPLOYMENT

The total size of the working population has changed relatively little since the Second World War. The Fifties saw comparative stagnation, followed by fairly constant growth, reaching a peak in 1974. The economic crisis then triggered a slight decline up to 1980, followed by a sharper decline between 1980-83.

Between 1983 and 1986, employment began to show an upward trend again. Statistics from the R.S.Z. (social security for employees) indicate that the number of wage-earners employed in the private sector increased by 34,000 over 1985-86. This evolution is largely due to the increase in part-time employ-

ment. R.S.V.Z. (social security for the self-employed) figures show that the number of self-employed also increased by about 10,000 in 1986.

But this brief summary is not the whole story: there were also important internal changes behind these developments.

The most obvious and characteristic of these changes was the decline of the agricultural population. The total number employed in industry hardly changed until 1974, but thereafter it was to feel the full force of the economic crisis, and employment in industry dropped by nearly 30 % in the space of 11 years. Almost all sectors suffered, but

the most hard-hit were the primary metallurgical industries, metal processing, textiles and clothing.

Employment in both commercial and non-commercial services (administration and education) shows a steady growth curve which has hardly been affected by the crisis. In fact, in the field of non-commercial services there is evidence that the pace of growth has actually accelerated, helped by measures introduced to combat unemployment. The number of self-employed is also declining: jobs lost in agriculture, trade and the crafts have not been compensated by the growth of the liberal professions and other specialist fields.

Nevertheless, the number of self-employed has been on the increase since 1983, partly as a result of measures introduced to encourage the unemployed to set up this sort of activity.

Finally, if the statistics are split into separate categories for men and women, a slow growth curve emerges for the male working population up to 1974, followed by a downward trend reflecting the successive job losses caused by the crisis.

The increase in the number of working women is much more pronounced and has scarcely been affected by the crisis.

But unemployment among women has

risen much more steeply than unemployment among men. The latter is mainly due to the reduction of the workforce through job losses, closures and rationalisation as a result of the crisis, particularly in industry. Unemployment among women, however, derives mainly from the great influx of women on the labour market, which could not provide enough jobs fast enough. A variety of sociological and economic factors are prompting more and more women to seek paid employment: in the Sixties about 23.5 % were professionally active, as against over 33 % in 1985.

INCOME DISTRIBUTION AND FAMILY SPENDING

Since the Second World War, the distribution pattern of national income over the various different income categories has changed radically. Wage-earners saw their share in the national income grow from 54.2 % in 1953 to more than 73 % in 1980, and then down again to just under 70 % in 1985. The proportion of the national income earned by agricultural workers plummeted from 6.2 % to 1.9 %, as a result of the even sharper drop in employment in this sector: the number of jobs in agriculture in 1953 was exactly four times the number available in 1985.

The share of tradesmen and craftsmen in the national income also continued to decline, while profits from private enterprise (private companies, dividends and reserves) rose initially from 5.5 % in 1953 to 7.4 % in 1970, and then went into a gradual decline, reaching their lowest level (3.5 %) in 1980. After 1980, income from private enterprise began to look up again, and in 1985 it had already risen to 8.4 % of the national income.

Another significant factor is the growing importance of unearned income from property and particularly from investments over the last ten years (1975-85), a phenomenon which is certainly linked with the explosive growth of the national debt and the interest payments this entailed.

SWEEPING CHANGES IN FAMILY SPENDING TOO

Private consumption shrank from almost 80 % in 1953 to just over 60 % in 1985. At the same time, the burden of direct taxation and social security contribution which families had to pay to the state more than doubled during the

same period, rising from 13.5 % of the family income in 1953 to 28.8 % after 1985. Savings followed a more irregular development curve, first moving upwards until they represented 13.5 % of the family income in 1970 and then gradually falling back to 8.9 % in 1985.

THE BELGIAN ECONOMIC SYSTEM

Like all other West European countries, Belgium has opted for a market economy. However, state intervention has become more and more frequent over the years, making it perhaps more of a mixed economy.

The following are some examples of state intervention:

1. Transport and communications are run mainly by state-owned companies: the railways, urban transport services, postal services, telecommunications, ports etc.

2. In the field of energy, production, transport and distribution are mainly in the hands of private sector companies, except for the import and transport of natural gas, which is run by a mixed enterprise.

However, the energy sector is controlled by a number of institutions with a tripartite structure including representatives of the government, the trade unions and the employers.

3. In the field of finance, there is a substantial public lending sector. The 'Société Nationale de Crédit à l'Industrie', the ASLK-CGER Bank, 'Crédit Communal de Belgique', 'Caisse Nationale de Crédit Professionnel' are public institutions that take in savings and extend credit in more or less specialised fields. The more recent 'Nationale Investeringsmaatschappij' and the 'Gewestelijke Investeringsmaatschappijen' (national and regional investment banks) were set up to provide risk capi-

Belgium has a centuries-old tradition in the textile trade. After a serious crisis, the textile sector made a dramatic recovery at the beginning of the eighties, due partly to extensive automation. The Belgian textile sector today is actually crying out for more skilled workers!

tal for private enterprise. The private banks fall under the supervision of the Banking Commission, which is responsible for the surveillance of the savings banks and public sector subscriptions in share issues.

All these financial institutions are subject to a system of tripartite consultation similar to that set up for the energy sector.

4. In the field of investment, a series of 'economic expansion laws' were passed from 1959 onwards. These laws introduced investment incentives in the form of low-interest loans, capital subsidies, loan guarantees and fiscal incentives geared to promote and reorientate regional investment in the various sectors. At a later stage, the crisis prompted more substantial interventions from the government in favour of sectors and enterprises in difficulties. This aid was often in the form of participations, with the state therefore also playing an entrepreneurial role in industry.

5. Then there are the export subsidies, which are designed primarily to make credit for large-scale export more competitive, and subsidies for research and development.

6. Prices are subject to a system of control which is applied more or less stringently, as required. The original system of prior notification of projected price increases gave way with the devaluation of the Belgian franc in 1982 to a price freeze, which was later eased to a certain extent when permission was granted for some price increases. From April 1987 onwards, various sectors or subsectors were gradually decontrolled.

7. Finally, the state has taken far-reaching intervention measures to promote the redistribution of incomes, through direct taxation, parafiscal measures and the social security system. The total sum raised in Belgium from these three sectors together amounts to about 45 % of the GNP.

In comparison with most other West European countries, government intervention in Belgium in the manufacturing and services sectors is fairly limited, except for the matter of price control and the redistribution of income. Nevertheless, there is a growing trend towards privatisation in our country, as elsewhere. The focus here is on improving the efficiency of the sectors in which public and joint public/private enterprises also operate, and on easing the pressure on the budget by reducing or eliminating operating losses in public enterprises as well as losses incurred through other forms of transfers to public or mixed enterprises.

Another important question facing the Belgian economy over the last few years is the maintenance of a competitive position, which is essential in an open economy like our own if we are to provide more employment opportunities and a higher level of welfare. Other priorities include getting the state finances back on a healthy footing, and easing the burden of taxation and other compulsory contributions which weigh mainly on earned income.

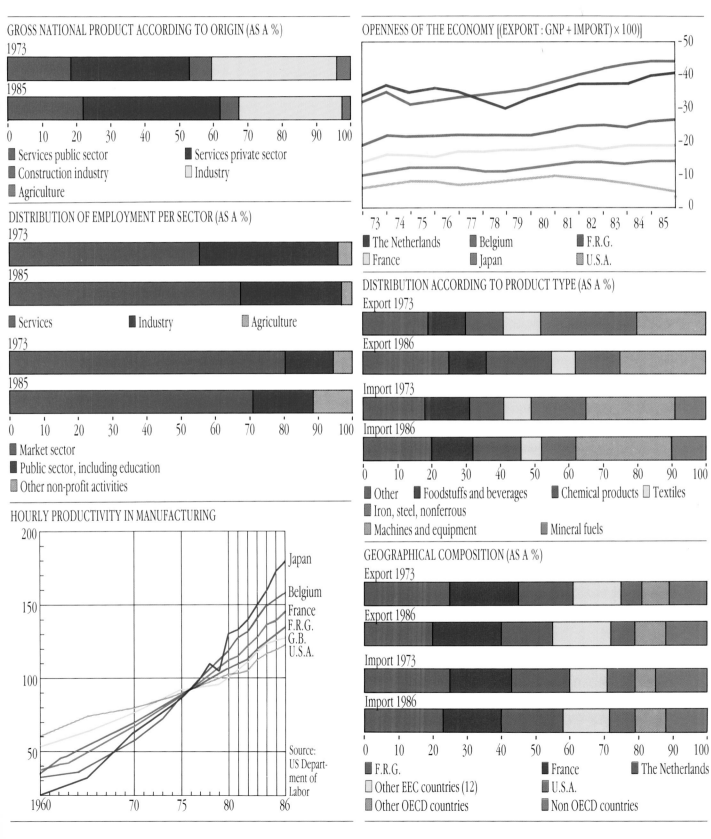

GROSS NATIONAL PRODUCT ACCORDING TO ORIGIN (AS A %)

1973

1985

0 10 20 30 40 50 60 70 80 90 100

■ Services public sector ■ Services private sector
■ Construction industry □ Industry
■ Agriculture

DISTRIBUTION OF EMPLOYMENT PER SECTOR (AS A %)

1973

1985

■ Services ■ Industry ■ Agriculture

1973

1985

0 10 20 30 40 50 60 70 80 90 100

■ Market sector
■ Public sector, including education
■ Other non-profit activities

HOURLY PRODUCTIVITY IN MANUFACTURING

200

150

100

50

Japan
Belgium
France
F.R.G.
G.B.
U.S.A.

Source:
US Depart-
ment of
Labor

1960 70 75 80 86

OPENNESS OF THE ECONOMY [(EXPORT : GNP + IMPORT) × 100]

-50
-40
-30
-20
-10
- 0

73 74 75 76 77 78 79 80 81 82 83 84 85

■ The Netherlands ■ Belgium ■ F.R.G.
□ France ■ Japan ■ U.S.A.

DISTRIBUTION ACCORDING TO PRODUCT TYPE (AS A %)

Export 1973

Export 1986

Import 1973

Import 1986

0 10 20 30 40 50 60 70 80 90 100

■ Other ■ Foodstuffs and beverages ■ Chemical products □ Textiles
■ Iron, steel, nonferrous
■ Machines and equipment ■ Mineral fuels

GEOGRAPHICAL COMPOSITION (AS A %)

Export 1973

Export 1986

Import 1973

Import 1986

0 10 20 30 40 50 60 70 80 90 100

■ F.R.G. ■ France ■ The Netherlands
□ Other EEC countries (12) ■ U.S.A.
■ Other OECD countries ■ Non OECD countries

35

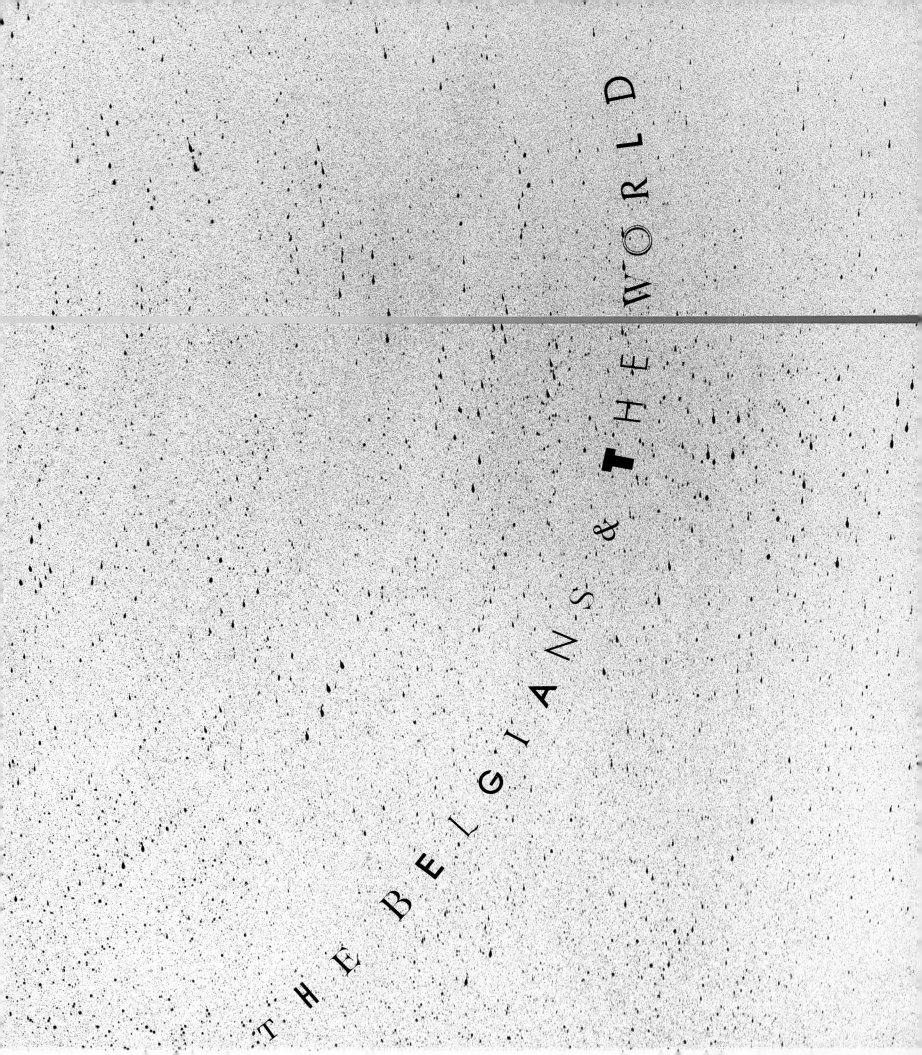

THE BELGIANS & THE WORLD

THE DIPLOMATIC HISTORY OF BELGIUM

ETIENNE DAVIGNON

THE PLAYTHING OF EUROPEAN DIPLOMACY UP TO 1830

Paul-Henri Spaak once said that Belgium had no foreign policy options: its only choice was to do what it had to do well or badly. A tiny country located at a nerve point of Europe, in which two different civilisations endeavour to rub along, Belgium is conditioned by all that happens outside its borders. Just as each moment in history is conditioned by the preceding moment, so it is with the diplomatic history of Belgium which in fact dates back to the Treaty of Verdun (843) disposing of the kingdom of Charlemagne. Bounded on the one side by France and on the other by Germany, delimited by and locked in the vice-like embrace of these two powerful giants, a third nation emerged — the Kingdom of Lotharius I, 'Lotharingia'.

Lotharingia was fated soon to vanish from the political map of Europe, to the benefit of its larger neighbours, in a welter of small, separate states springing up between the 11th and 12th centuries, none of them marked by strong central government, however.

The Belgian provinces were from early times viewed by their powerful neighbours (first France and the Holy Roman Empire, then in the 19th century, Britain) as the most sensitive, and hence most coveted, nerve centre of northern Europe for strategic, geographical and economic reasons.

The history of the 'middle kingdom', consigned by its position to the role of buffer state, has been one of repeated annexation attempts by its neighbours. Cast in the role of barrier, its fate was to be a turbulent — often dramatic — one, settled more often by the clash of arms than the negotiation of treaties.

A web of political and trade links was spun from the Belgian provinces very early on to the four corners of the known world.

This state of affairs continued for some four centuries, earning the provinces — coveted for their wealth and fertile soils — repeated invasions, almost always rebuffed as the would-be conquerors found themselves faced not only with the local town and village militia and cavalry — fired by traditions of independence and staunchly individualist — but also with the military might of neighbouring powers, unwilling at any price to see our lands dominated by a hostile power.

The chess-board of European diplomacy was thrown into total confusion in the 14th century by the rising political fortunes of the Burgundian dynasty. A Capetian family endowed with the appanage of Burgundy, it was to embark on a process of marriage alliances which, within the space of a century, would turn it into one of the most powerful — and certainly the wealthiest — dynasty in Europe. It was not long before the House of Burgundy made the provinces of what is now Belgium the hub of its European domains.

It was also seeking to turn the buffer role occupied by the provinces between France and the Empire into a keystone of its policy.

Feudal loyalty and close-knit family alliances — particularly enduring in the Belgian provinces — enabled the Burgundian dynasty, through a combination of inheritance, purchase and machinations, to carve out for itself a domain unequalled in wealth and variety. Indeed, it was only with the Ancien Régime at the close of the 18th century that the idea of unquestioning loyalty to the 'natural prince', first crystallized in the 10th century and over nine centuries thereafter often subsumed in the concept of patriotism, died out in Belgium.

The essence of that principle was the acceptance by his subjects of the sovereign's lawful authority by right of birth, in exchange for the reciprocal recognition by the Sovereign of his subjects' rights — a matter of bitter contention throughout the Middle Ages down to modern times.

In 1447, Duke Philip the Good saw that the historical situation might be exploited as a means of reuniting his scattered domain (Burgundy, the present-day Netherlands, Belgium and Luxembourg, including the neutral and complaisant ecclesiastical principality of Liège) with the addition of Lorraine and the fiefdom of Bar. Six centuries on, the name 'Lotharingia' resurfaced alongside the idea of a 'middle kingdom', posing a potential threat to the great powers of the period. It was in pursuit of this plan that Philip's son, Charles the Bold, was to perish at the battle of Nancy in 1477 leaving as his sole heir his daughter, Mary. Her marriage to Maximilian of the Austrian Hapsburgs, the Holy Roman Emperor, marked a decisive watershed in the long history of Belgium. The former sovereign States of the Low Country provinces, brought within the Burgundian fold, were

One of the most well-preserved castles with a moat in Belgium is the Gravensteen in Ghent.

henceforth to profess their loyalty for the next three hundred years to the Hapsburgs, as their 'natural princes'. The 'middle kingdom' came under the sway of its powerful neighbour, the Holy Roman Empire, condemning it to as many centuries of repeated attacks from the other neighbouring powers. The issue of this union, born in Ghent, the capital of Flanders, was to be the heir to the greatest empire of his time, Charles V.

Viewing with disquiet first the Holy Roman Empire, then Spain, jostling her northern borders, did France, through Richelieu, attack under the guise of recovering its 'natural frontiers' which included the Rhine to the north. This in turn aroused British fears of a French conquest of those provinces it considered the most sensitive for British interests in continental Europe. The Spanish Hapsburgs ruled from Madrid until the line was extinguished in 1700, and the ensuing War of the Spanish Succession saw the culmination of that bitter struggle between the great powers for the domination of the Belgian provinces rend Europe asunder for almost 15 years. The Treaty of Utrecht (1713) endeavoured to satisfy some while appeasing others: if the Spanish crown were to pass to Louis XIV's grandson, then the southern provinces would revert to the Hapsburgs, — but to the junior, Austrian branch. The 'Catholic Netherlands' (so described after the separation of the protestant Northern Netherlands from the catholic South, officially recognised by the Treaty of Munster (1648) after a protracted war) were henceforth known as 'the Austrian Netherlands'.

Throughout three centuries of Hapsburg rule, Belgium found itself not the nerve centre of the State, as under the Burgundian dynasty, but rather at the periphery. This frontier role, directed

to the north against the reformed Netherlands and to the south against French expansionist aims, and whose fall to either posed a potential threat to England, merited the Belgian provinces more than ever their nickname of 'the cockpit of Europe'.

These provinces, devoid of natural frontiers, ever open to invasions, were to experience more than their share of wars, massacres, depredations, occupations and pillaging. Incorporated by Charles V in 1543 into the empire as a new political entity, the so-called 'Burgundian Circle', the Low Country provinces increasingly began to discover the commonalities concealed beneath their individualism and jealously-guarded particularities. In addition to a common Sovereign, the people shared identical and complementary interests, the same urban civilisation had flowered for centuries along the courses of their great waterways, the relations between the Sovereign and his subjects were regulated by similar institutions in each province. Indeed, it was the duchy of Brabant which, in the 14th century, succeeded in establishing what might be called our first constitution — the charter of the Joyeuse Entrée (the 'Joyous Entry') — recognizing the reciprocal rights and duties of citizens and their lords. Similar charters soon became the norm in other principalities, creating a neatly-balanced political climate in which Brabant could develop.

At the close of the 18th century, the misguided ideas of the 'enlightened despot', Emperor Joseph II, in seeking to break with the — sometimes outmoded — traditions of his Belgian subjects, coupled with the shock-waves of the French Revolution and a fresh incursion by the invading forces of revolutionary France, sounded the final death-knell for nine hundred years of

gradual development towards the separation of powers, and brought to an abrupt end nine centuries of legitimist rule by 'natural princes'.

For the first time in their history, the Belgian provinces as a whole found themselves first subjugated, then annexed, by a foreign power claiming right of conquest.

The fall of the Belgian provinces into French hands caused profound disquiet among the neighbouring powers (including England), who had no wish to see such a nerve centre under French domination. The Powers began to muster their forces against France.

Waterloo (perhaps the most celebrated of all battles, and fought on Belgian soil), brought an end to French control of the Belgian provinces. The 15 years which followed (1815-1830) served to prove the unworkability of the structure forged by the Congress of Vienna concerning Belgium. For the statesmen of the Congress had regard only to the age-old role of Belgium as a bulwark and, in attaching it to the southern provinces of the Netherlands, had sought to create an immense buffer state between France and Prussia in the form of the newly-created Kingdom of the Netherlands administered by William I of the House of Orange-Nassau. Two centuries after its partitioning, the provinces of the Netherlands had finally been reunited. Two centuries in which, however, the Northern and Southern Provinces had forged sharply contrasting cultural, national, religious and individual identities. And the subsequent actions of William I showed him as maladroit a ruler as his precursor of 30 years earlier, Joseph II. History began to repeat itself. The Belgian Revolution of 1830 was sparked off by a heady mood of patriotism, amid the disarray among the signatory States to

the Congress of Vienna, once again discomfited by the prospect of seeing Belgium swept within the embrace of one of the major powers, once more to compromise the delicate balance of power in Europe constructed after the defeat of Napoleon. The Congress of Vienna had decided that, where the balance of power was threatened by any new development, the Big Five would take action to restore order by force. But 1830 was a year of ferment for Europe. In Paris, insurgents overthrew the absolutist monarchy and replaced it with a constitutional one, while Poland also sought to cast off the Russian yoke. The interventionist principles so carefully crafted by Metternich at the Congress of Vienna could not be applied, since the troops dispatched by the Czar to subdue the Belgian revolution were diverted to restoring order in Poland, while Prussia and Austria had their own uprisings to deal with.

The great powers were opposed to the Belgian revolution and the recognition of Belgian independence as a matter of principle. The only exception was the recently-enthroned 'King of the French', Louis Philippe, to the extreme annoyance of the other powers who had no wish to see France re-establish a foothold in the Belgian provinces, for it was not without good reason that Napoleon had remarked that: 'Antwerp is a pistol aimed at the very heart of England'. But Louis-Philippe stepped up his diplomatic lobbying for recognition of Belgian independence.

For its part, England was not displeased at seeing the United Provinces of the Netherlands shattered, for Holland's economic vigour (the seafaring northern provinces and manufacturing in the south) and its rate of commercial and industrial expansion threatened England's own primacy as both a European and colonial power.

After the secession of Holland in 1830 and up to the accession of the first Belgian king, Léopold I, in 1831, the young Belgian State was led by the 'Provisional Government'.

Belgian independence was finally decided by a Decree of the Provisional Government, issued on 4 October 1830, subsequently ratified, then proclaimed by the National Congress on 18 November 1830. On the following 20 December, the Powers, meeting in London, recognized Belgian independence — immediately qualifying it, however, by the Protocol of 20 January 1831 declaring Belgium 'perpetually neutral' under the 'guarantee' of the Five Powers: France, Britain, Prussia, Austria and Russia. This guaranteed neutrality finally laid to rest the thousand-year old spectre of a Belgium absorbed by one of its powerful neighbours and turned by it into a bridgehead against the others. The Lotharingian reality of Belgium as a bulwark gave way to the new political fact of a Belgium whose neutrality was guaranteed by all. The balance of power in Europe had been preserved.

The Belgian Constitution, framed from 1830-1831, incarnated a wholly original fusion of two currents of political thought and aims: on the one hand, the new ideals propounded by the liberal philosophers, and on the other an undeniable baggage of principles which were the legacy of a long and constantly changing historical tradition: the principle that all powers reside in the Nation (Article 25 of the Constitution), and are supervised and guaranteed by a constitutional, hereditary (male) monarch.

The selection of the first King of the Belgians was to prove a masterpiece of diplomatic and dynastic engineering, wholly acceptable to the great powers

French, thus offering assurance to France and guaranteeing the neutrality imposed on the country by the Powers.

INDEPENDENT BELGIUM

With Belgian independence recognized by the powers, the first task before Belgian diplomats was to negotiate the frontiers of the fledgling State, more especially those separating it from Holland. The Conference of London was to settle in outline exactly how the new Kingdom was to be severed from the Netherlands.

The negotiations proved to be labyrinthine, and the key role played in them by Mr Nothomb cannot go unacknowledged. On 26 June 1831, the plenipotentiaries agreed a treaty known as 'The Eighteen Articles', accepted by the Belgian National Congress but rejected by Holland. It was then, while Belgium was celebrating the enthronement of King Leopold, that William I chose to invade the country in a campaign which became known as 'the Ten Days'. Without the resources necessary to rebuff the invaders, the new King was obliged to call on France and England to fulfil their obligations under the Protocol of 20 January 1831 to act as a safeguard to Belgian neutrality. Guarantees were forthcoming from both Paris and London but the British government was naturally highly concerned by the entry onto Belgian soil of an expeditionary force under Marshal Gerard. The Dutch troops were compelled to retreat before the French force which, in effect, preserved Belgian independence. Thereafter, it required all the political skills of King Leopold and the Belgian diplomats to secure the withdrawal of the last French soldier from Belgian soil by 30 September of the same year.

The weakness of Belgian resistance dur-

The Siege of Antwerp by the French troops in 1831 (the 'Ten Days' Campaign').

ing the Ten Days led to a very marked hardening of attitudes among the European powers to the new Kingdom, chiefly manifested in the subsequent negotiations over what became known as 'the Belgian question' — in other words the country's borders. What clearly emerged throughout the negotiations was a very marked desire by the powers to maintain Belgium in the role which it had had for centuries past — that of kingpin in the balance of power in Europe.

The Conference of London resolved to put an end to the Belgo-Dutch dispute through a final and binding settlement, known as 'the Treaty of Twenty-Four Articles', published on 14 October 1831. This treaty reneged to a large extent on the provisions of the previous 'Treaty of Eighteen Articles'. Belgium's borders were set much as we know them today, and the country's independence was recognized in perpetuity. It required all the skill of the Belgian negotiators to steer the agreement through Parliament. With Parliamentary approval, Sylvain van de Weyer signed the Treaty on 15 November 1831 with the Plenipotentiaries of the five Powers. In the course of the Parliamentary debate, Mr Nothomb had remarked: 'Belgium, once formed, will be a vital country with a future. It will

never perish, because Europe's word is its bond'. The following decades were to bear out the truth of his statement.

The general tenor of the Kingdom of Belgium's foreign policy was thus made clear, and it was to the great credit of the early monarchs — who kept a firm hand on the tiller of national diplomacy — that they appreciated how the essential principle of neutrality could be tempered by subtle manipulation of the guarantor Powers to enable Belgium to very gradually claim its place on the international stage.

At the very outset, diplomatic activity naturally focussed on the loose ends resulting from the scission of the Netherlands and Belgium, chief among which ranked the problem of indebtedness and the free navigation of the River Scheldt. During this time, the new State was unfortunately limited in what it could do by an economy in ruins. Independence meant Belgium also had to seek out not only a stable manufacturing base, but also fresh ways of selling its output to foreign markets. That was a delicate task, but one successfully accomplished by clear-thinking individuals, despite the obstacles posed both by Parliament and public opinion, too easily and too often swayed by a misguidedly idealistic picture of the true state

while providing the kingdom with a well-respected royal house. For the future King of the Belgians, Leopold of Saxe-Coburg-Gotha, product of a German royal line and related to the Czar of Russia, was the husband of the late heir to the English throne and was living in England at the time of his election by the National Congress. Once on the throne, he was to marry the daughter of Louis-Philippe, King of the

King Léopold I (1831-1865)
King Léopold II (1865-1909)
King Albert I (1909-1934)
King Léopold III (1934-1951)

of the nation. It is not superfluous, however, to say that sound Belgian common sense triumphed in the end.

The Treaty of 19 April 1839 between Belgium, Holland, the five Powers and the German Confederation, signed in London, was a milestone in laying the foundations of the new Kingdom. At the same time, Belgium was developing its diplomatic relations, covering the globe with a network of consuls whose job was to expand the openings for foreign trade.

The Treaty of 1839 was followed by a period of rapprochement in Belgo-Dutch relations, with the chief stumbling block being the negative — if not downright hostile — attitude of William I of Holland towards Belgium. The prospect of Belgium becoming a member of the German Confederation and the Zollverein was mooted. The government of France made strenuous efforts to bring Belgium within the sphere of French influence. And throughout the period, England jealously watched over Belgian neutrality, which enabled it to preserve the balance of power in Europe.

1848 was a watershed year in the history of Europe, with few states escaping some form of revolutionary ferment, doubtless riding the coat-tails of what

was dubbed 'the industrial revolution'. Belgium remained relatively unscathed by social unrest, but to preserve social peace intact, the Government was obliged to be particularly attentive to relations with neighbouring states, themselves in the throes of violent change, or looking to turn the clock back to the pre-Congress of Vienna position, or even with thoughts of annexing our fledgling state.

Belgian neutrality was once more sorely tried by the Franco-Prussian War of 1870.

Belgium secured from Prussia the same promise as that given by France, but a promise subject to the French Empire's honouring of its undertakings towards Belgium. The two belligerent nations reserved the right to enter on Belgian soil in defence of its neutrality if the other were to advance into it.
The legitimacy of such a claim could not be disputed, for neutrality had been established not simply in the interest of Belgium, but of Europe as a whole.

It became clear — particularly to King Leopold II — that peace in Belgium was necessarily contingent on its remaining neutral, but that diplomacy alone no longer sufficed to guarantee that neutrality. Thus developed the Kings's abiding concern to buttress the

country's foreign policy with a credible military defence capability capable of discouraging any thoughts of incursion into Belgian territory.

The diplomatic communities of Europe naturally continued the diplomatic waltz at the end of the 19th century. Each state recognized Belgian neutrality, and schemes proliferated, in many of which Belgium was the bargaining counter — but each time, the balance of power in Europe consigned them to history. This was the climate in which Leopold II was able to pursue his grand diplomatic design culminating in the Conference of Berlin (1885), the outcome of which was to put under Belgian rule that immense swathe of central Africa known then as the Congo, and today as Zaire.

The 20th century had barely begun when an event so apocalyptic in the history of nations sparked off a process which was to change the face of the international community beyond all recognition.

The 1914-18 War was, in fact, the first throes of an upheaval which, in time, was to radically change the balance of power, awaken all parts of the globe to the fact of life as part of an international community, and spur a dizzying pace of advance in science and technology; in

short, it was to usher in a new form of society. And it was Germany which, in flouting Belgian neutrality, triggered off the process. The war which ravaged Europe was to become a world war whose four-year duration was to wreak radical changes to the international community. Power relations would never be the same again. When the dust settled, Belgium was on the side of the victors, and its resistance had earned it considerable international prestige. The Treaty of Versailles, signed on 28 June 1919, officially recognized King Albert's renunciation of the status of perpetual neutrality of November 1918. The King had needed all his powers of persuasion during the negotiations to secure recognition of the country's rights from the 'Big Three'. Among the concessions obtained by Belgium were adjustment of its eastern borders, the right to reparations from Germany, a presence in the Allied force of occupation of the Rhineland, and membership of the League of Nations. Failure to make the reparation payments led to Belgium and France jointly occupying the Ruhr in January 1923.

Belgian diplomats were actively involved in redrawing the ground-rules of the new balance of power. Belgium also intended playing a full part in the League of Nations, with all its efforts directed towards assuring peace through diplomatic channels rather than by force of arms. This is illustrated by the Locarno Pacts of October 1925, by which Belgium, represented by its Minister of Foreign Affairs Emile Vandervelde, saw the official abrogation of its status of imposed neutrality. The frontiers between Belgium, France and Germany were recognized and guaranteed by Italy and Britain. The signatories undertook to settle their differences by international arbitration. Armed force would be used only in the event of an attempt by Germany to reoccupy the demilitarized zone of the Rhineland established by the Treaty of Versailles.

The 1930s were marked by the world slump of 1929 and the rise to power of Hitler in Germany. Belgium, concentrating on developing its interests in the Congo, gradually awakened to the need to pay closer attention to developments in its next-door neighbours. The German army's reoccupation of the Rhineland in March 1936 was a particularly rude awakening. With its security under threat, Belgium asked for further mutual guarantees from France and Britain under the Locarno Pacts. Neither country wanted any truck with it, leading the Foreign Minister of the time, Paul-Henri Spaak, to advocate a 'wholly and utterly Belgian' foreign policy. On 14 October 1936, King Leopold III set out the broad lines of the Kingdom's foreign policy, namely, independence as part of a voluntary neutrality supported by a military policy strengthening the country's defensive capability aimed at preventing war on Belgian soil and distancing Belgium from the conflicts between its neighbours.

What Belgium was seeking for itself was a status of guaranteed neutrality which, unlike the pre-1914 neutrality imposed on it by the Powers, was decided by Belgium itself in full sovereignty. After a flurry of diplomatic activity, the French and British governments recognized Belgium's declared neutrality on 24 April 1937, and undertook to maintain the 'engagements of assistants' previously taken towards it. A similar declaration was made by the German government on 13 October 1937.

The clouds of war loomed larger, however. The echoes of the Spanish Civil War reverberated across Europe and Germany's claims became ever more strident.

Belgium redoubled its efforts as a peacemaker. On 23 July 1938, the Foreign Ministers of Belgium, Holland, Luxembourg, Denmark, Finland, Sweden and Norway agreed a Convention in Oslo proclaiming the common ideal of their countries as peace, impartiality and a commitment to avoiding all forms of armed conflict. It was a vain attempt by the smaller European states to change the course of history. Events gathered speed. The Belgian government called another meeting of the 'Oslo Group' in Brussels on 23 August 1939 in a renewed and touching call to preserve peace. On 28 August 1939, King Leopold III of Belgium and Queen Wilhelmina of Holland offered the German, Polish, French, British and Italian governments their 'good offices' in an endeavour to avoid war. The offer was repeated on the following 7 November to the German, French and British Heads of State. On 10 May 1940 Belgium, its 'guaranteed' neutrality in shreds once again, was drawn into the Second World War.

The war was barely over before the Belgian government took steps to give a fresh slant to Belgian foreign policy with the signing in London of the Benelux Treaty in 1944 — an option confirmed after the Liberation and the resumption of 'normal working' for the institutions of government. Belgium had taken its first steps along the road towards international cooperation.

Twice betrayed by its policy of neutrality, and twice within less than a quarter of a century obliged to rebuild its economy, Belgium drew the lessons of its failures and resolved that, better than being a pawn in the precarious balance of European power was to become a champion of international solidarity — a solidarity made all the more necessary in the eyes of Belgium's foreign policymakers by the war's destruction of European hegemony in the world. It was also becoming increasingly manifest that events in the different continents were linked by cause and effect, and that development of the mass media and communications was now at such a pitch that the world had been reduced to a global village.

On a world level, then, Belgium laboured to make the United Nations as effective an organization as possible in its peacekeeping role and keep it free of the obstacles which had paralysed the League of Nations in the inter-war years.

Having pleaded in vain against granting the major powers a right of veto, the Belgian government consistently advocated the search for a balanced arrangement allowing each nation to state its case. And while it had to be acknowledged that the great powers perhaps had more rights than the smaller ones, the reverse side of that argument was that the great powers also had more onerous duties towards the international community than did the smaller nations.

Belgium's aim was and is to make a positive contribution in all institutions of the United Nations system, be it the General Assembly, UNCTAD or the specialised agencies. One may wonder whether the volumes of paperwork produced by these bodies are not simply too theoretical and abstract. That may be a reasonable contention, but the question also remains whether the United Nations has not been instrumental in bringing substantial changes and progress to the contemporary world. Among the achievements to the United Nations' credit are the East-West talks, the North-South Dialogue and the process of decolonisation — not, perhaps, in having found answers to them, but assuredly for having prevented serious

The Monument in Bastogne to the memory of the American soldiers who fell in the German offensive on the Ardennes in the winter of 1944-45.

ETIENNE DAVIGNON

situations from deteriorating into all-out wars.

On a regional level, the same commitment to international cooperation has repeatedly driven Belgium to be among the founders of associations — both Atlantic and European — as a means of coming closer to attaining its goals. The Brussels Treaty paved the way for the pact with North America, from which was to emerge the Atlantic Alliance, guaranteeing the defence of — and hence peace in — this region of the world. For the Belgian government, this political alliance was to go far beyond its purely military dimension to become, during the 1970s, an instrument of East-West détente through the 'Harmel Plan'.

The Council of Europe was the focus of the immediate post-war hopes of European federalists. And while it may not have quite fulfilled all its early promise, it did serve as the instrument for Franco-German rapprochement. With the European Convention for the Protection of Human Rights and Fundamental Freedoms, the Council of Europe rekindled one of the strong points of European civilisation by restoring the defence of the individual as one of the chief concerns of nation-states.

The pursuit of its foreign policy objectives, underpinned by a belief in interdependence, was also what drove Belgium to participate in the various schemes to build a united Europe. The Treaties of Paris and Rome stand as a monument to that. Belgian diplomacy has often been decisive: without the Spaak Committee, there would have been no Treaty of Rome to compensate, in part, for the first great failure in European integration: the European Defence Community. Paul van Zeeland, Pierre Harmel and Leo Tindemans also

took often-decisive initiatives for the development of the European Community. The Belgian Government has been consistently concerned to redress any imbalances likely to arise between Member States through institutional machinery, giving each state its due responsibilities within the organization in order to prevent any one Member State from unilaterally imposing its will on the others. The role of the Commission within the European Communities, and the weighted voting rules in the Council of Ministers, attest to that concern for balance coupled with effectiveness.

Preserving peace, protecting human rights, providing decent living conditions, maintaining trade, assuring a fair distribution of wealth and a stable monetary system, bringing nations closer together and confronting the challenges of the future: such are the constant tasks and abiding aims of Belgian foreign policy.

THROUGH THE AGES

Throughout history, Belgians have left home to roam the world for a multitude of reasons, driven to do so, indeed, by the internal dynamics of the Belgian provinces which (along with northern Italy) saw the earliest flowering of a European trading — and hence urban — culture, constrained by its nature to a ceaseless quest for new markets. The Hanseatic League was to see countless merchant mariners setting out from Bruges to furrow the seas of Northern Europe.

Yet others, impelled by self interest, were able to turn the know-how acquired in the Belgian provinces to profitable use elsewhere. like the 15th century Flemish weavers taking their skills to Scotland and northern England.

From the 15th century, craftsmen were not only to be found in riverside settlements for the links with outside markets, but also in the royal courts of the world. Thus it was from Flemish artists that the Italians learned the technique of oil painting, destined to supersede the overly delicate, destructible 'fresco' techniques.

It was also in the 15th century that foreigners took to describing all things artistic and commercial from the Belgian provinces as 'Flemish', and all things military and industrial as 'Walloon'. Hence the Tournai-born Roger de la Pasture never shook off the title of 'Flemish painter', while the Hainault musician Roland de Lassus was later described at the court of Spain as a 'Flemish musician'. Likewise, the troops recruited in the Belgian provinces for the Spanish royal militia were always described as the 'Walloon guards', regardless of the region they came from. The 16th and 17th centuries witnessed a steady forced exodus of Belgian converts to Protestantism, obliged to flee

for their lives into exile: they found sanctuary chiefly in the Netherlands, Scandinavia (where Walloon craftsmen introduced the art of iron working to the lasting profit of Swedish manufacturing industry), and even as far as the United States, where the first governor of what was later to be New York was the Hainault-born Pierre Minuit.

At the same time, fervent Catholicism drove many Belgians to throw themselves with missionary zeal into the footsteps of the great explorers. Their reputation for perseverance and unshakeable belief was undisputed: it was Saint François-Xavier who, dispatched to convert the Japanese and dying in sight of the islands, wrote to his superior in Rome, 'above all, send me Belgians'. That missionary zeal has never flagged, and this provided the Catholic church with evangelists the world over, like the Reverend Father De Smet, sent to convert the American Indians; the Reverend Father Verbiest, followed by Father Lebbe, in China; or Reverend Father Damien, whose flock was the leper colony of Molokai. And the later Belgian missionary work in central Africa still remains one of the largest-scale undertakings ever achieved by the Catholic Church.

That many far-flung lands were explored from the 16th century onwards is largely a tribute to the work of Belgian cartographers, working to information provided by their fellow citizen/adventurers: what schoolboy is not familiar with the names of Gérard and Rumold Mercator and Plancius ?

But for Belgium, overseas involvement was truly to begin in the 18th century, when the Ostend Company was founded by the Austrian government with a charter giving it 30 years of privileged trade with Africa and the East Indies, together with the right to found colonies.

But it was the reign of Leopold II that witnessed the real expansion of Belgian interests overseas. And its unlooked-for success was the result of a series of interlocking, but individually crucial, factors: the imperative need to find new markets for the country's steadily-growing manufacturing output; the commitment to making Belgium a hub of industrial processing, leading to a paramount need to locate (and if possible acquire) new sources of raw materials; the emergence of an aware political commitment to both aims, with a resolute determination to extend Belgian influence abroad, to which the life and reign of Leopold II were a monument; and finally, from 1880 onwards, the flow of Belgian private capital, by now a force to be reckoned with, but too frequently deployed in purely domestic ventures, towards a broad span of investments in foreign countries in the classic form of (often highly profitable) 'venture capital' investments.

But hand in hand with the financial aspect went philosophical and humanitarian considerations, such as the evangelising role of the Church, and the spirit of adventure burgeoning in the nation's youth.

But perhaps the real driving force behind the worldwide migration of Belgians was that Belgium, considered a 'modern' country for its time, in the vanguard of technical, scientific and administrative efficiency, and with few of the ambitions of the great colonial powers, was frequently called on by developing nations to provide supervisory personnel to nurse through radical changes in the widest variety of sectors: thus Belgian police were found maintaining law and order in Macedonia; Belgian civil servants helped reorganize the main public services for the Persian Empire; Belgian lawyers held top administrative posts under the

King of Siam, and organized the courts of mixed jurisdiction in Egypt; and yet other Belgian civil servants helped reform public administrative agencies in Chile and Bolivia.

While 1880 saw Belgians begin to make their imprint on the world, it was unquestionably the 25 years from 1890 to 1914 which saw the movement attain its first zenith with ventures which — for the time — were nothing less than successive waves of an industrial revolution, with such as Edouard Empain responsible not only for Heliopolis in Egypt, but also for the design of the Paris metro, and the success story of Solvay, whose celebrated ammonia-soda process was popularised through his 25 factories worldwide.

Emile Francqui was to secure the concession to build the Peking-Hankow railway, whose 1,215 kilometres would require 120,000 labourers working under the general supervision of Jean Jadot, a veteran of railway building in Belgium and Egypt. China was also to award the Tien-t'sin concession to Belgium, which, through a variety of companies, including the Banque Sino-Belge, an associate of the Société Générale de Banque, was to play a key role as an economic motor.

Eugène Sadoine opened up vast markets in the Russian Empire for the Cockerill factories, followed by Evence Coppée, precursor of the modern coal and coke industry; their pioneering led to the presence of some 30,000 Belgian workers housed in villages with names evoking their homeland dotted around the Russian capital of St Petersburg.

Georges Nagelmackers was to found the Société des Wagons-Lits, which operated the celebrated Orient Express; while Rolin Jaequemyns was to put the finishing touches to the modernisation of Siam. In an entirely different field,

Statue of Léopold II in Ostend.

Opposition from the other European trading nations, however, led to the charter being suspended in 1731.

Essentially, it was not until the early days of the fledgling kingdom that Belgians systematically ventured overseas as part of a grand commercial design: for it was then that a plan for the nation superseded purely occasional adventures, attributable to separation from the southern Netherlands, the stirrings of nationhood and the need to discover new outlets for Belgian industry now deprived of the shipping facilities offered for the past 15 years by the Dutch merchant fleet.

The credit for having hit at a very early stage upon the need for Belgium to lay worldwide trade bases as a foundation for its exporting future must without doubt go to King Leopold I, who had, moreover, come to see that a degree of emigration might go some way to solving the acute problem of poverty riding the coat-tails of Belgium's industrial revolution. That is one reason why, for instance, organized — and sometimes subsidized — Belgian colonial settlements were found springing up all over the United States, such as in Wisconsin, Pennsylvania and Indiana (where one village was called simply 'Léopold').

Adrien de Gerlache was to rise to fame as the leader of an expedition south of the Antarctic circle, conquering the South Pole in March 1899.

Many of these prestige-winning ventures were underpinned by a sound grasp of technology: Belgians were responsible for the construction of railways in Turkey, Argentina and Mexico, and the electrification of Rio de Janeiro and Sao Paulo. Not infrequently, however, this went hand in hand with a romantic but hard-nosed vision of the future and the avowed aim of making a return on capital invested.

It was considerations of this order, indeed, which moved Léo Baekeland to emigrate to the United States after bringing his research into the prop-erties of plastics to a highly advanced stage in Belgium. Faced with total indifference in his homeland, he set his cap at the New World where he immediately took out and began to work the patent for what he called 'bakelite' — his success speaks for itself.

But Belgian vigour also permeated the world in a host of other fields beyond the diplomatic, technical and economic spheres: in politics, the influence of the Second International spread, and the voice of socialism, speaking from Brussels through such as Vandervelde and Huysmans, was heard and heeded everywhere; the practitioners and philosophers of Art Nouveau spread the word across Europe and America; social reforms essayed by Belgium were taken up by an increasingly wide circle of other nations.

BELGIUM AS A COLONIAL POWER

From the 1880s, however, the main thrust of Belgian external development focussed on central Africa — more particularly in the Congo, over which Leopold II's personal sovereignty was recognized by the other powers in 1884. This purely personal union was ratified by the Belgian Parliament, but the Congo was not to become a Belgian dependency until 15 January 1908. The first task set for themselves by Leopold and his hand-picked Belgian administrators was to rid the land of the slave-traders whose annual bloody plunder-ing of the area decimated the villages along the caravan route from the Congo Basin to East Africa. The new philanthropic crusade was launched by Cardinal Lavigerie from the pulpit of the Collegiate Church of Saint Gudule, Brussels, in 1888. The campaign to suppress the slave trade, with Dhanis at its head, was strongly supported by the native populations, and was completed in 1893 with the total routing of the slave-dealers and traffickers.

Leopold II's grand design was now set to take off, and would determine the Belgian attitude to Central Africa, thereby setting Belgium on a path to a destiny previously undreamed of.

Businessmen, administrators, military leaders and missionaries all put their

In the 19th century, Belgian engineers built railways all over the world: in China, Iran, South America and other countries — and of course in what was then the Belgian Congo.

shoulder to Leopold's wheel with a commitment which helped allay the doubts, even then being voiced in Belgium, about 'colonial adventures'.

Medicine and hygiene were the first priorities: physicians had been numbered among the earliest campaigners to stamp out the slave trade; and 1895 saw the founding of a network of institutes and laboratories throughout the Congo, initially concerned with vaccination, and later with the study of tropical diseases. In 1906, Leopold decided that a school of tropical medicine should be established in Brussels (relocated to Antwerp in 1936) for the compulsory training of all doctors wishing to practice in the Congo. In 1983, the Institut de Médecine Tropicale Prince Léopold (Prince Leopold Institute of Tropical Medicine) awarded its one hundredth certificate...

As early as 1908, Dr Broden had suggested using missionaries as paramedical staff, leading to the award of diplomas in tropical medicine to many priests and nuns bound for central Africa.

It was this fusing of the medical and missionary efforts which was to turn the Congo by 1920 into the 'grid of chapels and dispensaries' noted by all observers. An administrative plan for the gradual introduction of a medical system began to take effect from 1931 onwards.

In 1960, the World Health Organization acknowledged the density and exceptional quality of the medical services introduced by the Belgian authorities into the Congo, making it the best-equipped country for medical facilities in central Africa.

Natural mineral resources were discovered early in what was to become the Belgian Congo, and were exploited in

flexible and innovative ways: through such things as the creation of the Compagnie du Katanga (1891), management of the mining sector by the Comité Spécial du Katanga (1900), the granting of extensive mining concessions as a quid pro quo for risks incurred by railway companies (CFL in 1902 and BCK in 1906), the setting up of Forminière and the Union Minière du Haut-Katanga, the organization of the national mines of Kilo-Moto and the formation of the Comité National du Kivu (CNKI), mineral resources played a major role in the prosperity and development of the Congolese infrastructure; bolstered the 1940-45 war effort with the supply of strategic raw materials, and now continue to contribute to the prestige of Zaire among former colonial territories.

And behind all these achievements stand the massed ranks of Belgian geologists, technicians and investors who, with the help of the local workforce, were able to optimize the mineral wealth of central Africa.

Even today Zaire remains the leading world producer of cobalt, the fourth largest of cadmium, and thirteenth in importance for zinc.

Belgian engineers were quick to lay the foundations of the first railway network and by 1889, at the behest of Leopold II and spurred on by Albert Thys, the Matadi-Leopoldville (Kinshasa) line was opened, playing a key role in the suppression of the slave trade and spelling the end of the use of bearers.

This led to the construction of the longest and most diversified railway network in central Africa, an undertaking continued today in the present Republic of Zaire. At the same time, the 12,000 km of navigable inland waterways were opened up for combined rail/waterborne transport.

This infrastructure was also destined to serve the interests of Belgian investors, the largest of which, Société Générale de Belgique, did not allow its core activity of mineral resources development to stand in the way of other investments in selected industries or shipyards.

This chapter in Belgian history should not be closed without noting that the Belgian way of getting things done, with its characteristic dynamism and empiricism, had led the Allied Powers

to make a rare gesture: when the German Empire's colonial possessions were dismembered after the 1914-18 war, two of the states adjacent to the Congo — Rwanda and Urundi (Burundi) — formerly under German sway were put under the trusteeship of Belgium. And the accession to independence by the Congo (now Zaire) in 1960 was followed in 1962 by the attainment of self-government for both trust territories.

It would not be difficult, given time, to catalogue the darker side of the Belgian presence in central Africa. All nations have skeletons in their closets. Despite that, for a small country with no history of colonial experience, armed only with their beliefs (be they political, missionary or economic) and their collective will, the Belgian achievement was both significant and laudable. And their efforts were to be projected into modern times through other methods and to more universal goals: cooperation for development.

BELGIAN DEVELOPMENT COOPERATION

What exactly do we mean by that amorphous term 'development cooperation' — that venture in which Belgians have taken an active and unflagging part, and which it is all too easy to imagine that we understand, so deeply has it become ingrained in the fabric of international relations, to the point where it has spawned an entire network of national and international institutions?

Its objectives and strategies have evolved over time, shaped both by economic and political circumstances, and changing perceptions of the needs of what Alfred Sauvy first called, and is now generally known as, 'the Third World'.

On 30 June 1960, the Belgian Congo was granted independence. King Baudouin, with the first President of the new Republic, Kasavubu.

In the early days, concerns were directed toward helping newly-independent states by providing them with technical assistance — an area in which many Belgians were able to contribute valuable experience.

The inadequacy of that approach soon became manifest in a world waking up to the fact of interdependence, but one where rich and poor nations still rubbed elbows. And it was not long before the less well-off states began to raise their collective voice to demand that the balance be redressed.

The moral and humanitarian duty to aid the less fortunate, which alone warranted a positive response from the wealthier nations, was not the sole reason behind the implementation of increasingly varied development cooperation programmes. It was clear to all that solidarity between rich and poor was paramount, for both stood to benefit from it. Who could fail to see that the economic development of the Third World was an essential precondition to the development of trade, creating wealth for both alike? And who could close their eyes to the fact that injustice, misery and hunger were a source of tension and conflict which endangered the major patterns of trade?

But agreement on to ultimate ends did not automatically imply a consensus on the means of getting there.

Students on the campus of Lovanium University in Kinshasa (Zaire).

Any discussion on a problem of such complexity cannot but be intricate. And the issue is far from being closed even now, although the successes and failures of the strategies implemented do enable us to take stock of it in a way which might help to achieve a closer meeting of minds.

The task is, admittedly, an immense and multifaceted one. Sometimes,

indeed, it is the very survival of the most at-risk populations which has to be striven for through such things as emergency aid to combat famine, epidemics and other natural disasters. But other than such exceptional situations, each individual must be given the capability of feeding himself and provided with basic health care. But even that is not enough. We must build a future in which each country can pursue its own development standing on its own two feet; which means eradicating illiteracy, training technicians and managers, providing agricultural and industrial production technology, creating administrative, financial and economic infrastructures, but also reshaping the structures of the world economy.

Belgium's traditions fitted its people well to contributing to this task. The Government equipped itself with the necessary instruments. A Minister was given special responsibility for development cooperation, with the resources of a central department at his disposal — the Administration Générale de la Cooperation au Développement (AGCD - General Administration of Cooperation for Development - GACD). The financial resources available to the Minister are supplemented by contributions from other government departments. Belgian aid to the Third World is not confined to the admittedly broad-ranging activities of the GACD.

Before turning to the other forms of Belgian cooperation, a brief look at how the GACD deploys its activities might be in order.

The GACD acts on a bilateral basis, directly by sending out technical cooperation assistants on assignment, through the carrying-out of studies, work and execution of integrated projects, awarding study fellowships, granting food and emergency aid, and via fi-

nancial assistance. Studies, works and integrated project execution are commissioned by the GACD from properly-equipped private sector firms.

The GACD acts indirectly by calling on the services of non-governmental organizations (NGOs) to which it provides financial backing, as it also does to universities initiating their own educational schemes geared towards development cooperation.

Although the GACD provides bilateral aid to over a hundred countries, the lion's share still goes to Zaire, Rwanda and Burundi. Which shows the enormous breadth of the problems to which fitting solutions must be found. Priorities have to be set on a regional basis: rural development and its related activities in sub-Saharan Africa, the transfer of technology, know-how and training in the more advanced economies of the Maghreb, South East Asia and Latin America.

The strategies and machinery of cooperation, if it is to be both dynamic and effective, must also be capable of accommodating acquired experience and adjusting to changing circumstances. Thus, it became clear that ad hoc projects did not necessarily lead to the expected economic growth, which is, in fact, dependent on the interplay of a variety of factors. In future, therefore, the GACD seems likely to place an increasing emphasis on programmes integrating complementary projects falling clearly within the development priorities set by the beneficiary country.

A versatile financial instrument was also needed to enable new methods of financial cooperation to be initiated. That came in the form of the Fonds de la Coopération au Développement — the Development Cooperation Fund. These new forms of intervention were

designed to meet the needs of equal partners, individually responsible for the administration of their own development programmes. The financial arrangements available range across a broad spectrum, from lines of credit at lower-than-market rates, to the acquisition of equity interests in national or regional development banks, and even in semi-public companies.

These new methods clearly reflect the Belgian concern with ensuring that its development cooperation ventures grow out of a dialogue and decisions arrived at jointly with the beneficiaries of aid, whose responsibility it is in the first instance to set the goals and priorities of that cooperation.

Noteworthy in this respect is how frequently the dialogue is not confined simply to the two countries involved, but increasingly encompasses the international institutions whose task is to assist the economic and social development in the Third World. The GACD magnifies the 'knock-on' effect of this type of operation by co-financing arrangements with the World Bank and the regional development banks, with many of which it has an equity link. None of this should come as a surprise.

The comparatively slender means available to a country such as Belgium are not sufficient to enable it alone to foot the entire bill for the financial and human resources required by some large-scale projects.

That is not to say, however, that the strictly Belgian component of aid for projects carried out in harness with international institutions is insignificant. On the contrary, the size of the Belgian contribution to many projects has been a decisive factor. The creation of the Fonds de Survie belge (Belgian Survival Fund) with an authorized expenditure commitment of 10 billion Belgian

francs (a figure which speaks for itself) in response to the appeal on 28 June 1981 from 77 Nobel prizewinners to combat genocide by starvation and under-development, stands as a fine example of Belgium's role as prime mover and the quality of its cooperation with international agencies, for it was the IFAD, in alliance with the WHO, UNDP and UNICEF, which found itself cast, by agreement, in the directing role of field operations coordinator.

The Belgian contribution to the multilateral development cooperation effort is not confined to the GACD's contribution to the budgets of regional and multilateral financial cooperation funds and programmes such as the EDF, FAO, IFAD, WFP, UNICEF, UNDP and a host of others. For Belgium has always been an active supporter of and participant in the European Economic Community's development cooperation effort, the pioneering work of which has become a byword.

This brief bird's eye view of the many facets of the Belgian commitment to the effort to afford all peoples of all nations not only decent living standards, but ones offering scope for future development, would be lacking if special mention were not made of the country's resolutely receptive stance to the concerns of developing countries in discussions in the specialised international forums on such major problems as the freeing of trade and reducing the levels of their foreign indebtedness.

By way of conclusion to an overview which may give some idea of the actions of the Belgian government and its people throughout the world, but cannot hope to do them full justice, perhaps their attitude can be summed up as:

1. committed, constant involvement;

2. a quest for effectiveness in routine matters springing from a pragmatic approach to problems;

3. a dogged and unshakeable commitment to international institutions — the only system by which today's highly interdependent world can be administered;

4. a determination to advance the cause of an integrated European Community — the sine qua non of the economic and political development of our continent;

5. labouring through Atlantic solidarity to strike a balance which will assure peace;

6. the quest for more fairness all round through observance of the law and assistance for development.

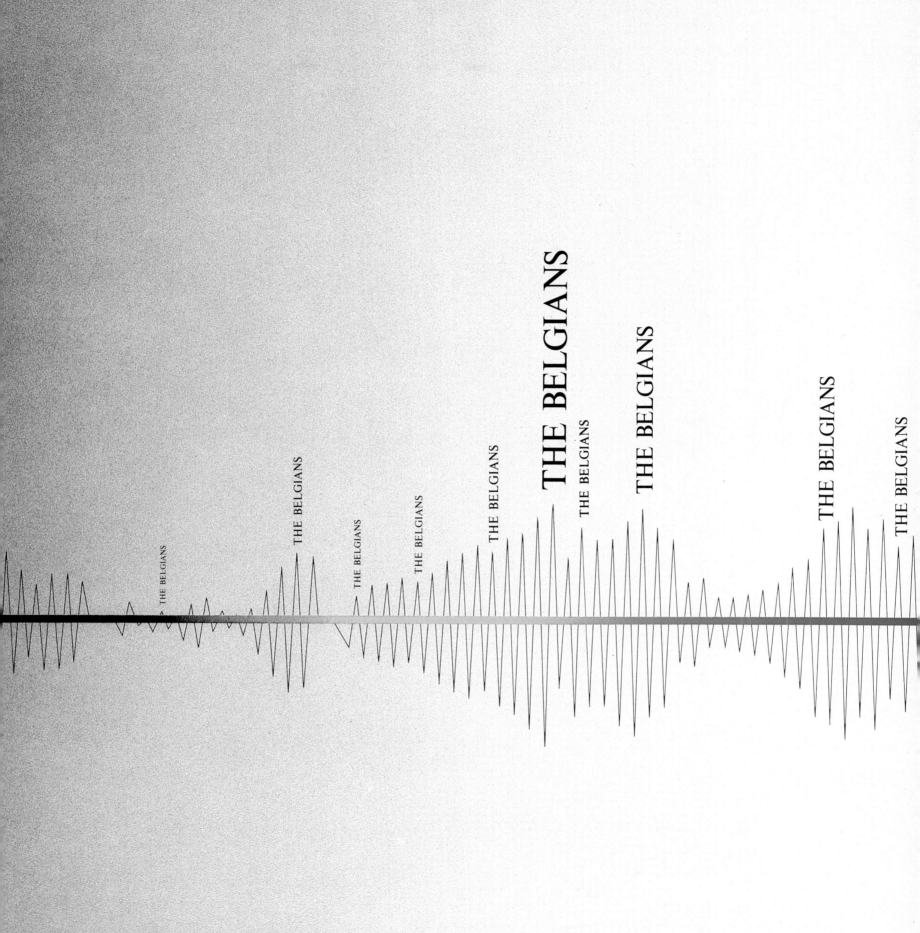

THREE PEOPLES AND ONE STATE

JOHAN FLEERACKERS

The beautiful Beguinage of Bruges has inspired many an amateur painter.

DIVERSITY

The language conflict and painting are often the two key concepts which the generally well-informed media drum into the foreign visitor as soon as he sets foot in Brussels or anywhere else in Belgium. How characteristic are these elements of the real Belgium?

The people of Belgium do seem to have painting 'in their blood', and they like to hear themselves described as a nation of painters. Proof of this lies in the many museums, the scores of art academies, galeries and auctions, the walls of private living rooms displaying 'all our own work' and the serried ranks of amateur painters, even including ministers of state, who immortalise this pleasant land — and sometimes themselves — on canvas for posterity. Belgium is proud of its artistic past, and not without reason, as other sections of this book will show.

The first step towards understanding social and political life in Belgium is realising that it is a microcosm of Western Europe. Belgium has grown up in the border region overlapping the Latin and Germanic cultures. The invisible cultural boundary, which has been laid down in Belgian law as the language frontier, was established in the early Middle Ages and has remained remarkably stable ever since. This linguistic frontier has no geographical landmarks, but it is an eloquent demonstration of profound differences in human geography. Wallonia and Flanders have different population densities and a different style of living, different statistical patterns of births and deaths, and different age structures in their populations, different agricultural methods and different crops, a different industrial climate and of course, a linguistic and cultural dichotomy. Industrial development and the media have not had any profound effect on these differences.

Trade relations between North and South are very intense, but social contact between the two communities is weakening. In the bilingual capital, Brussels, where the national state departments are concentrated, there is permanent contact between the two linguistic groups. But Walloons and Flemings live independent cultural lives for the most part, which is surprising within such narrow territorial limits.

One of the reasons for this is that the circulation of newspapers, magazines and books, as well as radio and television programmes, is more or less limited to the language area concerned, although there is more interest in Flanders for literature in other languages.

The fact that there is so little social intercourse between the two main communities of Belgium does little to help understanding on a national level. The Flemish community has the demographic upper hand, with about 59 % of the total population of Belgium: but in Brussels, a variety of historical, political and sociological circumstances have made the Francophones the dominant majority, accounting for between 75 % and 90 % of the population of the capital.

52

The Belgian coast is a favourite among holidaymakers from Belgium and abroad.

The revision of the Constitution in the nineteen-seventies and eighties rounded off the sharpest consequences of these demographic relationships in the structure of political decision-making: the Belgian government was to be formed on the basis of linguistic equal representation. In practice, tolerance is the order of the day. The spirit of democracy can be seen, not so much in the high-flown rhetoric on a national level, as in the practical compromises of daily life which keep it alive.

Foreign visitors are often surprised at the extreme exactitude with which our complex legislation defines the linguistic and cultural rights of the three communities, and at the fact that all central state administrations are divided into twin single-language departments or bilingual departments, right down to the literal translation of the briefest notice pinned up in the government buildings of the capital. These language laws are the fruit of a difficult but always peaceful search over the centuries for a solution acceptable to all within a democratic system of law: few other states have been able to emulate Belgium in its non-violent handling of an emotionally-charged and irrational question like ethnic relations.

THE ART OF LIVING

A country is more than the sum of its political institutions, export figures, church towers and museums. The character of a community shows more clearly in people's spontaneous reactions to day-to-day events, and in how human relationships work in practice. In this country too, the business of daily life is the citizen's prime concern. The high rate of unemployment, any threat to the health of the nation (and the environment), freedom from care in old age, peace and security (especially close to home) have top priority in the list of human hopes and desires. For the average Belgian, high ideals are worth fighting for if there is some chance of achieving them. There are no quixotic heroes in Belgian literature, but on the contrary a Tijl Uilenspiegel, a charismatic realist with a touch of cynicism in his outlook on life.

If self-knowledge is the beginning of wisdom, the Belgian approach is perhaps not far wrong: not placing undue importance on being right, putting one's own achievements in perspective rather than boasting about them, because truth is relative, a feeling that being right is only useful if one can convince others of one's rightness, and that one's own contribution is only valuable until someone else produces something better. Belgium no doubt owes this gentle cynicism to its history.

For centuries, Belgians have been aware that many things will be decided above their heads and that whether they like it or not, their own personal efforts are unlikely to change the course of events significantly. History has also taught the Belgians to prepare carefully for the future. The national urge to save is powerful, and savings are mainly channelled into the classic

Belgian investment: a home of one's own. Although prosperity has increased fourfold in the space of half a century, memories of poverty and austerity are still kept alive by family tales of grandmother's day. The prosperity boom in the sixties led to large-scale over-consumption, even in the private sector.

The Belgian ability to reach a compromise is legendary, and this consummate skill can be seen in action in the way in which major political and social problems are resolved through compromise in this country, often after virulent argument, street demonstrations, parliamentary debates, diatribes in the press and government crises. At the height of the argument, the opponents often abandon the conference table to adjourn to a select restaurant, for the Belgian cuisine is renowned for its quality, and Belgians are known for their readiness to do justice to it, and moreover, it is well-known that a good meal is a great persuader. Many a national dilemma, social conflict or industrial dispute has been solved in a matter of hours over a glass or between the courses. So, dear reader from abroad, beware: the restaurant is a tender trap where the Belgian will persuade you how right he is — or almost.

The Belgian family circle will only open its doors to an outsider after very careful selection, because for many, the family remains a 'safe house' where privacy is guaranteed and feelings can be expressed spontaneously. A newcomer will only be welcomed into the family circle if the acquaintanceship has taken on a more personal dimension — and this can take a little longer than usual in other countries. But once a friendship has reached this stage, the hospitality will be full and unreserved, built to last a lifetime. Comfort in the home is among the best in Europe, and

The Nature Reserve in Genk.

home cooking, too, is a delight for the palate. The vast majority of Belgians enjoy an annual holiday, and the summer migration to the sea, the Ardennes and southern Europe is on a grand scale. The remarkably high concentration of hotel and tourist accommodation, especially in the Flemish coastal resorts and the richly forested Ardennes, makes Belgium a favoured holiday destination for many visitors from abroad the whole year round.

Leisure activities and sport still account for a large proportion of spending in Belgium. From time immemorial, football and cycling have been the

favourite spectator sports of both Flemish and Walloon sport lovers. Many a world cycling champion has been a Belgian, for Eddy Merckx was not alone. Substantial state investment in sport has stimulated active participation in almost all branches of sport today: judo, tennis, horse riding and even the very select sport of golf are all gaining popularity daily.

Belgium is above all a land of clubs and associations, where every inhabitant over the age of 50 has been chairman of a club at least once, whether it be a club for social work, culture, sport, charity or simply a social club. For the

foreigner living in Belgium, it will often be rather more difficult to find an opening in that finely-woven and often apparently impenetrable tissue of typically Belgian 'brotherhoods'. These associations draw their membership mainly from one language group, except in the case of some clubs in Brussels. But anyone wishing to get to know the living folklore of the Belgian people, religious, comic or historical, should keep an eye on the calendar of annual processions and parades, some including effigies of the traditional giants (the Holy Blood Processions of Bruges and Nivelles, Veurne's Penitents' Procession, the Procession of the Cats in Ypres etc.). And in at least one town in each linguistic area (Binche, Aalst and Eupen), the annual carnival is an opportunity to meet the Belgians in a unique mood, with their reticence thrown to the wind in wild abandon.

THE BELGIAN IDENTITY

The question of whether Belgium is inhabited by one or three distinct ethnic groups often sparks off eloquent debates among Belgians. A hundred and fifty years of cohabitation has given Belgium a unique national culture of its own, in which many Walloons, Flemings and Bruxellois still feel at home — although they may not admit it in public... This common Belgian identity is of a different order than the regional folk culture which is built on a centuries-old heritage, but it is an equally important sociological reality. Nevertheless, although this national feeling is less patriotic, less chauvinistic in Belgium than elsewhere in the world, a Belgian can pick out a compatriot amongst millions, and recognise him as such, especially in time of war and trouble — or when bumping into him abroad.

In spite of language differences, and in spite of an increased regional awareness, many aspects of life and social behaviour in Belgium are still subject to a common, national influence: town and country planning, the style of living, dressing, eating, recreation, sport and leisure activities, education and jurisdiction, politics and religious life. There is indeed a Belgian way of life, which is the product of 150 years of shared experiences, full of intercultural characteristics which an outsider will immediately identify as national characteristics or 'typically Belgian'.

This lifestyle is influenced daily by contact between commuters on their way to the capital, between the masses of

spectators at football matches and pop concerts, and among the countless clients surging in and out of the great departmental stores: all aspects of Belgian life which are organized on a national level.

So the national consciousness is broadening in two directions: both inwards on a regional or subnational level and outwards beyond the frontiers of our small fatherland. There are signs that a growing European awareness is gradually emerging in certain areas of society and especially among the young, together with an increasing feeling of being part of the whole world — 'the world is my village'.

There is also a growing awareness that European society is evolving towards a multi-cultural and multilingual community. Brussels is one of the outposts of this irreversible trend. In some neighbourhoods of the capital, residents are mainly foreign, and in some municipalities on the outskirts, more than 30 nationalities rub shoulders. Integrating these new elements harmoniously with the old, grafting these different lifestyles onto the existing sociocultural structure, and reconciling them with the historical rights of the linguistic and cultural communities: all this is a difficult process. Experience in Belgium has shown how a failure to recognise linguistic and ethnic aspirations at the right time can seriously undermine national solidarity and even the structures of state. In this context, the adaptation of Belgian public institutions to meet regional aspirations is an important political experiment which European observers would do well to follow closely.

BELGIUM:
THE CENTRE OF A MEGALOPOLIS

To visitors from another continent, Bel-

gium looks like one great agglomeration, where brilliant town planners and architects have laid out long ribbons of streets, houses and mansions among parks, gardens, woods and meadows. A charming exaggeration perhaps, but not without an element of truth. With almost 10 million inhabitants in an area of just over 30,000 km^2, Belgium is one of the most densely populated countries in the world. But it has no huge metropolitan cities. The agglomerations of Brussels, Antwerp and Liege with 1 million, 500,000 and 200,000 inhabitants respectively are cosmopolitan in character, but have still remained pleasant towns to live in. Travelling from one town to another rarely takes much more than an hour. Houses are built relatively far apart, and this is typical of land use in Belgium. Most Belgians share the ideal of owning a home and garden for one's family and friends, being born with the proverbial 'brick in the belly' — or the urge to build a house for oneself. And indeed, more than 65 % of all privately-owned houses are owner-occupied. This green agglomeration is the heart of the European 'megalopolis', the wide, urbanised area of north-west Europe including the German Ruhr with Cologne and Düsseldorf, the Randstad in Holland taking in Amsterdam and Rotterdam, the Parisian agglomeration and Greater London.

What the tourist remembers most about the countries he has visited is often the towns. But the Belgian landscape is one of contrasts, although referring to the Ardennes as the 'Belgian Highlands' is perhaps a bit fanciful, since the highest peaks are no more than 650 metres. Belgium summarises the landscape of Europe along the North Sea. The Ardennes and the high moorlands of the Hoge Venen in the south, along the

borders with Germany and the Grand Duchy of Luxembourg, contain a magnificent nature reserve where 'langlaufen' (cross-country skiing) is growing more and more popular in the winter. Central Belgium is an area of gently rolling hills gradually merging into the maritime plains of Flanders below, divided from the North Sea by a narrow strip of dunes. These 'lowlands by the sea' and the Flemish polders are part of the same geographical entity as the lowlands of Holland and Friesland, which have been referred to jointly for centuries as 'The Low Countries'.

Up to the Belgian independence in 1830, urban population remained stable. It was not until the second half of the 19th century that the population of the towns again began to increase, particularly with the opening up of the river Scheldt and the growth of industrialisation. While only 28 % of the Belgian population lived in the towns in 1831, by the turn of the century this had already grown to 50 %. Today, at least two thirds of the population live in urban agglomerations. The towns in the Walloon industrial basin saw the greatest urban expansion: Liège, Charleroi and Mons, as well as along the road between Brussels and Antwerp. These towns also saw the emergence of the first workers' proletariat, which was to have a profound effect on the course of the social and political history of the land. But an inborn sense of property, a dense railway network and the Belgian's historical attachment to his home village and his own region prevented a mass exodus to the cities. Flanders in particular remained a predominantly agricultural area, apart from Antwerp and Ghent, while in the Campine and the Ardennes there were only small industrial centres rooted in the region.

After the Second World War, a second

A wintry Sunday morning in Ghent.

wijk in Berchem-Antwerp, and the integral restoration of the Groot-Begijnhof (or Beguinage) of Louvain. Namur and Liège contain examples of the successful combination of restoration and integration architecture (St. Barthélémy - architect Ch. Vanden Hove).

The Regional authorities have since given absolute priority to the policy of urban renewal, and have introduced tax concessions designed to promote and subsidise the restoration of privately-owned monuments. But all these praiseworthy actions cannot make up for the many tragic mistakes of the past. And Belgium is not alone in this. While much of our heritage is being salvaged in the cities, historical monuments are disappearing in the villages and the countryside.

wave of urbanisation got underway. The Brussels area saw a particularly explosive expansion, which was intensified from the sixties onwards by the establishment of the EEC and NATO headquarters. Almost 10 % of the total population lives in Brussels, but in contrast with the top-heavy concentration of population in the capital cities of neighbouring countries, the demographic concentration in our capital is counterbalanced by a dense network of medium-sized towns and the postwar economic expansion of Flanders, particularly in towns like Antwerp and Ghent. Sixty percent of all buildings in Flanders date from after World War II, and a quarter were actually erected after 1970.

Against the backdrop of the growing suburbs, a gradual depopulation of the old inner city centres could be discerned in the sixties and seventies. This 'back to nature' movement was no doubt also influenced by factors like environmental pollution, land specu-

lation and increased mobility. But experts point out that the effect of this exodus of town dwellers was to accelerate the introduction of urban lifestyles to the country, gradually supplanting the traditional way of life, rather than the other way round.

Many towns had to pay a price for the post-war prosperity boom. Old residential quarters in historical towns were often demolished to make way for massive building projects. It was not until after 1968 that people began to feel a twinge of nostalgia for what they saw as their old paradise lost. This triggered a reaction among individual citizens, specialists and local authorities, who drew public attention to the matter and campaigned against the destruction of the centuries-old fabric of the cities. In 1975, the International Historic Monuments Year, 'Citizens' Action Committees' were set up all over the country. The Koning Boudewijnfonds (King Boudewijn foundation), which was established on the occasion of the

25th anniversary of his accession to the throne (1950), also channelled substantial funds into the restoration of the nation's forgotten or decaying architectural heritage. These actions had their effect, and in the space of a few years, the tide had turned. The rapid depopulation of the inner city areas of cities like Antwerp, Ghent, Liège and Namur has been held back or even reversed.

Living in the old town centres has become popular again, thanks to new legislation on the protection of historical monuments, and restoration and repair grants for the renovation of houses which have fallen into decay. All over the country, central zoning schemes have been drawn up and ratified, while in many town centres, pedestrians have been given priority again in new pedestrian shopping streets and precincts. Whole quarters have been listed as historic monuments and restored to be handed down to posterity unchanged. The most impressive examples of this are the protection of the Cogels-Osy-

Moves towards integrating architecture and urban planning still clash daily with sturdy individualism. The ubiquitous ribbon developments stretch out their tentacles from one village to the next, as one of the most characteristic features of the urbanised landscape in Belgium. The criticism of many urban planning theorists is not so much that there is no good architecture — which of course there is, with fellow-countrymen like the architects Horta and Van de Velde — but that there is no good planning, just the permissive chaos of 'laissez faire'.

The creation of the new university town of Louvain-la-Neuve deserves special mention. Building started just outside the little Walloon town of Ottignies in 1971. Original architecture has achieved a harmonious integration with the landscape, producing a stylish complex on a human scale. Louvain-la-Neuve was the first new town to be built in Belgium since the foundation of Charleroi in 1666.

THE RISE AND FALL AND NEW RENAISSANCE OF EDUCATION AND SCIENCE

JOHAN FLEERACKERS

HISTORICAL EVOLUTION

The evolution of intellectual life, education and culture in general has always followed the ups and downs of political, social and economic history throughout the ages. Belgium is a classic example of this. Our provinces enjoyed high renown in the intellectual world as early as the late Middle Ages and the Renaissance. The many monastery and abbey communities were the first centres of professional scientific work.

The foundation of the *University of Louvain* as the first continental university in north-west Europe in 1425 was an event of profound historical significance, and the university was to become famous throughout the transalpine world. Particularly from the 16th century onwards, spectacular results were booked in the field of science, with great names pushing back the frontiers of knowledge in Europe from Louvain within the space of one generation. Andreas *Vesalius*, born in 1514, was the founder of modern anatomical science, and was one of the first to study the human body on a scientific basis, breaking the taboo on human dissection. *Geeraerts Mercator*, born in 1512 and a contemporary of Vesalius, concentrated on cartography. His famous Mercator projection 'ad usum navigantium' made great intercontinental expeditions possible. His invention, which is still used in sea, air and space travel today, laid the foundations of the explosive growth of overseas trade. Rembert *Dodonaeus* or Dodoens, born three years after Vesalius (1517), was the first scientific botanist, Abraham *Ortelius* (1527-98) a famous geographer, Jan *van Helmond* (1577-1644) laid the foundations of modern chemistry and the mathematician and physicist Simon *Stevin* (1548-1620) established a system of scientific

nomenclature in the language of the people.

After this golden age, the pace of scientific progress began to slow down as a result of the succession of military expeditions and the religious wars of the 16th century. The recapture of Antwerp in 1585 by Farnese heralded a long period of political unrest, accompanied by the exodus of most intellectuals, men of letters and philosophers. The closure of the Scheldt and the decline of economic activity plunged the Southern Netherlands into a trough of lethargy in the late 17th century. This did not begin to change until the late 18th century, when an 'Imperial Academy of Science, Arts and Letters' was founded in 1772 under the reign of the Hapsburg Empress Maria-Theresia. During the same period, the *'Theresian Colleges'* were also established in the most important towns of the realm, and these were to give education a new impetus. The Enlightenment thus brought some glimmers of hope to the impoverished Southern Netherlands too, but under the Ancien Régime, education and science remained the domain of a small élite. It was conducted moreover mainly in Latin, and in social and intellectual life, Dutch had been completely ousted by French.

The socially progressive Brussels lawyer and politician Jan-Baptist Verlooy argued in the true spirit of the Enlightenment for the reinstatement of Dutch, the language of the people, in his impressive 'Verhandeling op d'onacht der moederlijke tael in de Nederlanden'. But in vain: a few years later, the Belgian provinces were annexed under the French Empire and the Dutch language was banished from public life completely. France's contribution to cultural life was however limited, except for the foundation of an 'Ecole de Musique' in Brussels in 1813.

As an enlightened sovereign, William I played a significant role in the restoration of education and science in the united Netherlands. As early as 1817, two new universities were founded in the South: the State Universities of Liège and Ghent. A Royal Music School was opened in Brussels in 1826, and a Music School in Liège. The education of the people was substantially improved, as was the syllabus and the professional standard of teaching staff. The first nursery schools were also opened during this period, though at this stage they were little more than child-minding centres. William I also ensured that primary school teachers should once again teach in the language of the people in the Flemish provinces. The short period of the United Kingdom of the Netherlands was to have a far-reaching effect on the maintenance of the Dutch language and culture in what later became Belgium.

A new generation of scientists emerged in the 19th century. They were encouraged and stimulated in their work above all by Lambert Quetelet (1794-1874), who was Secretary of the Royal Academy for more than 40 years. Within the space of a few years, the young state founded important scientific institutions and also took on the first scientific researchers in permanent service. It is an impressive list, and one which contrasts sharply with the intellectual lethargy of the previous two centuries. The years after 1860 were a period of particularly active organization of the sciences, with the foundation of the Royal Observatory, the Royal Meteorological Institute, the Royal Institute of Natural Science, agricultural centres, the Royal Library, the National State Archives and the Royal Belgian Fine Arts Museums. Most scientific institutions were housed in new, prestigious buildings designed ac-

cording to the spirit of the times as temples for the edification of the people. An equally important milestone was the reopening of the *Catholic University* (1834) and a few months later, the *Free University of Brussels* which based its teaching on the principles of doctrinaire liberalism and free research.

In the meantime, education had also been reorganized according to the new constitutional directive establishing the principle of free choice in the selection of schools. The framing of this directive and above all how it was put into practice later, was the result of a whole series of political compromises between the two main ideological movements in Belgium: the Catholics, who defended private sector education organized by the Church, and the free-thinkers, who supported the State-organized schools.

From 1874 onwards, scientific research expanded rapidly, especially at the universities, and almost all branches of science were involved in this expansion. However, a list of scientists of international renown would lack coherence and moreover fill up far too many pages.

The pioneering work of some of our compatriots in the field of medicine and physiology in particular achieved international renown. Nobel prizes were awarded to the researchers Jules *Bordet* (1870-1961) in 1919, to Corneel *Heymans* (1892-1968) in 1938, Chr. *de Duve* and A. *Claude* in 1974 and in 1979 to P. *Prigogin*. The Nobel prize for literature was awarded in 1911 to the Flemish man of letters Maurice *Maeterlinck* (1862-1949), who wrote in French. And finally, it is very characteristic that the Nobel prize for peace should have been won by Belgium three times, the last recipient being

The youth of Belgium: at the dawn of a new era, and exciting new challenges.

Father Dominique *Pire* in 1958, for his work as the founder of the 'peace islands'. This little country where so many armies have fought out their battles knows only too well how little is to be gained by war.

Compulsory education, introduced just before the outbreak of the First World War, was not implemented until five years later. At the same time, in 1921, the first measures were introduced for the democratisation of education. The 'Fund for the exceptionally talented', later the National Educational Fund, was set up to award educational grants to young people from the less privileged strata of society. Nineteen twenty-eight saw an important step in the development of science with the estab-

lishment of the *National Fund for Scientific Research* (NFWO), on the initiative of King Albert. The Fund is administered by representatives from the Universities, scientific institutes, industry and commerce, and other bodies and awards grants to young researchers. After the war more special funds of this type were set up, including the *Institute for the Promotion of Scientific Research in Industry and Commerce* (IWONL) in 1944, which performs an important function. The period between the wars was characterised by efforts to improve the content of educational programmes and above all by the political battle to establish *the Dutch language* as the official medium of instruction in secondary and higher education in Flanders. The University

of Ghent became first bilingual, and then in 1930 Dutch was established as its official language, followed shortly after by the Catholic University of Louvain (there was only one Catholic institute of higher education), which also set up separate Dutch-speaking faculties after 1932 in addition to the existing French-speaking faculties. Secondary education in Flanders, which was originally provided in both Dutch and French, used only Dutch as its teaching medium from 1932 onwards.

The period after the Second World War saw a new upsurge of important political/ideological discussions on the subject of education (1956), but attention was focused above all on the democratisation of higher education. Various

new universities were set up, for instance in Antwerp and Mons, and in Brussels, where an autonomous Flemish university (the VUB) was founded in addition to the existing French-speaking Free University dating from 1834. Various smaller university faculties were also created. The most remarkable achievement was the creation of the new French-language university in a completely new, custom-built *town* Louvain-la-Neuve, a few kilometres from the language frontier. The political complications attending this move continued to disturb the linguistic balance in scientific circles for many years. Its psychological effect was great, and accelerated the pace of administrative reform, the introduction of cultural autonomy for the three communities

(1970) and the constitutional reform of 1980. Other important innovations have also been introduced in education over the past decades: in addition to the democratisation of university entrance, decision-making structures in the universities themselves were also made more democratic. In the seventies, the *renewed secondary education* system was introduced, a reform designed to achieve a greater degree of interaction between the various disciplines and a widening of programme horizons.

Yet another significant development of this period was the growing participation of young women in higher education, catching up on centuries of lost opportunities within the space of a few generations.

The end of the Second World War was to have far-reaching effects on scientific research in Belgium, as elsewhere. After 1950, scientific research was directed more and more towards industry. The *study centre for nuclear energy applications* was set up as early as 1952, and various small and medium-sized companies established joint scientific research centres. Belgium also takes part in the most important international research centres like *Euratom*, the *European Atomic Energy Agency* in Vienna and the *Atomic Energy Research Centre* in Geneva, as well as participating in European scientific *Space programmes* (ELDO and ESRO). In addition, the regional executive governments have paid particular attention to the promotion of applied scientific research over the last few years. The technology exhibition *Flanders Technology* became an impressive international forum for the presentation of the most advanced innovations in the field of applied scientific research. The regional executive government of Wallonia, too, has succeeded in generating

Informatics are the key to the future for the children of Belgium too.

a creative and innovative climate through operation ATHENA, its activation campaign for the promotion of technology. More and more *joint ventures* are being undertaken by the universities and industry. Impressive results have been booked in the pharmaceutical industry and microelectronics in particular, making Belgium one of the international leaders in applied research.

THE VISUAL ARTS

PHILIPPE ROBERTS-JONES

FROM THE MIDDLE AGES TO THE 19TH CENTURY

Over the centuries, the area that is Belgium today has always been a crossroads where different cultures meet, a melting pot of ancient artistic traditions. Painting has pride of place here, but other art forms also have an important part to play.

The Middle Ages saw a remarkable development of the decorative arts, in the field of ivory work, gold and silverwork, and miniatures. In the 12th century, the Mosan school was known all over Europe, created masterpieces such as the magnificent baptismal font of St Barthélémy in Liège, between 1107 and 1118, and knew such artists as Rénier de Huy, Godefroid de Huy or Nicolas de Verdun. In the 13th century, Hugo d'Oignies carried on the tradition of gold and silverwork.

In the 14th century, the sculptors came to the fore, in Tournai and elsewhere. But the end of the century was dominated by the sculptor Claus Sluter from Haarlem, who worked in Brussels around 1380 before leaving for Dijon where he produced his 'Moses' Well', which was to influence the painters of the 15th century through its realism and expressive power. Tapestry-making blossomed, as did wall-painting, a few rare examples of which have survived. By the year 1400, the most important influences (Italian and French) converged in the international Gothic style, both in painting in general and miniatures, as can be seen in the book of hours *'Les très riches heures du Duc de Berry'* illuminated by the Limburg brothers.

But the era of the Flemish Primitives, so important in the history of art, did not dawn until the 15th century, with the rise of the economic and political power of the Burgundian state under Philip

the Good (1419-67). The great urban centres were also the centres of the art world of the time — Tournai, Louvain, Brussels, Ghent and Bruges. The corporate structure of the guilds helped the crafts to flourish and guaranteed the quality of the work. Jan van Eyck, who carried the technique of oil painting on canvas to new heights, triggered a revolution in the representational arts and opened the way to Flemish realism with his religous works like the *Mystic Lamb altarpiece* (1432) and the *Madonna with Chancellor Rolin*, and his portraits, like that of *Giovanni Arnolfini* and his bride.

The Master of Flémalle in Tournai, the creator of the triptych *The Annunciation* (Merode), was perhaps still influenced by the gothic sculptors, but he was already linking daily life with the divine. The highly religious art of his pupil Rogier van der Weyden — *The Descent from the Cross* (Escorial) and *The Last Judgement* (Beaune) — an artist who was born in Tournai and appointed official painter of the city of Brussels, became very popular and inspired many imitators throughout the century. Other great masters of this time were Dierick Bouts, painter of the famous *Justice of Emperor Otto*, Justus or Joos van Gent, a native of Ghent working in Urbino, Hugo van der Goes, whose dramatic works reflect his own restless spirit, and three painters working in Bruges: Petrus Christus, Hans Memling and Gerard David. All of these artists represent the formal and spiritual discipline of art focusing on religion and portraiture, each in his own style. In sharp contrast to this, there is Hieronymus Bosch of 's Hertogenbosch, with his own world of fantastic imaginings.

Flanders attracted countless foreign artists at this time, and their paintings were exported all over Europe. The same is true of sculpture and above all

the ornamental altarpieces created in the ateliers of Brussels and Antwerp, some of which have been discovered as far afield as Scandinavia.

In the course of the 16th century, which was dominated by the figure of Charles V who was crowned Emperor in 1519, medieval ideas began to give way to the new spirit of the Renaissance. Antwerp, with its port and flourishing commerce, became the most important centre. A rich variety of styles and movements developed in the art world: mannerism, realism and the fantastic, with artists like Quinten Metsijs, Jan Gossaert called Mabuse, Bernard van Orley, Joachim Patenier,

Pieter Aertsen and Joachim Beuckelaer.

While other artists of the mid-16th century were producing landscapes, genre works, and religious and mythological paintings, Pieter Bruegel the Elder was brilliantly combining the secular and the sacred, the real and the imaginary, the spirit of his native region and the spirit of Humanism. Bruegel developed into one of the greatest painters of his time, with works like *The Proverbs, Dulle Griet* (Mad Meg), *The Seasons, The Fall of Icarus, The Blind Men* and the *Magpie on the Gallows.* His style was widely imitated and his work was circulated mainly through engravings. The art of engraving developed from

The museums of Belgium have rich collections including works from all the important periods.

and technique. He was renowned in his time at all the courts of Europe for his religious and mythological canvases, his official and private portraits, and his great, lyrical landscapes, which made him a powerful influence right up to the time of Delacroix and Renoir.

Rubens' most important contemporaries were Antoon van Dijk, remarkable portrait painter and founder of the English school, and Jacob Jordaens, who painted religious, mythological and popular subjects. They emerge from a great number of talented landscape painters, portraitists and genre painters who applied themselves to still-life, animals and flowers at this time. Other notable artists of the period include Jan 'Velvet' Brueghel, Frans Snyders, Jan Fyt, David Teniers, Jacques d'Artois etc.

During the 16th century, tapestry-making developed further in Brussels under the influence of Rubens, and also spread to Antwerp, Edingen and Oudenaarde. Lace-making flourished in Flanders, the glass industry in Liège, leatherwork in Mechelen and gold and silverwork and diamond cutting in Antwerp. The sculpture of the age is to be found mainly in the churches, and the influence of Rubens can be seen clearly in the work of Lucas Faydherbe of Mechelen and Artus Quelien the Elder of Antwerp. A more Italianate influence can be seen in the work of the sculptors Frans du Quesnoy of Brussels and Jean Delcour of Liège.

In the 18th century, in 1719, the provinces which were later to become Belgium came under Austrian rule. The tradition of high quality art was maintained during this period, although no outstandingly creative artists emerged. However, some of these artists did enjoy success abroad, such as Jan-Frans van Bloemen and Pierre-Joseph

Redouté. Under the Empress Maria Theresa at the court of Charles of Lorraine, highly refined, classical art was practised by artists including the sculptors Gabriel de Grupello, Laurent Delvaux and Gilles-Lambert Godecharle. The latter was also a link with the next century.

The 19th century brought a new revival in painting. The French Revolution and the Republican campaigns put an end to the Austrian rule. Our provinces came under the sovereignty of France until it was replaced in 1815 by the Dutch rule of William of Orange. During this period, Louis David, a French exile, came to live in Brussels, together with his pupil Francois-Joseph Navez, who was to be one of the leading Neo-classicists.

FROM 1830 TO TODAY

In 1830, the Belgian State was born, and the same period saw the rise of the Romanticism of Gustaaf Wappers and Louis Gallait and above all the visionary artist Antoine Wiertz. This new development is nevertheless still linked with the deeply-rooted traditional realism, which blossomed again through the works of Joseph and Alfred Stevens and Charles De Groux. A succession of artistic societies was set up. The Société Libre des Beaux-Arts was founded in 1868, with members including Louis Dubois, Louis Artan, Félicien Rops and Constantin Meunier. Rops re-established the reputation of European engraving and Meunier overshadowed the sculpture of contemporaries like Kessels, Geefs, De Vigne and Van der Stappen with his working class subjects.

In 1883, the Les Vingt group was set up in Brussels on the initiative of Octave Maus. The annual exhibitions of this group included not only works by the Belgian avant-garde artists Guillaume

the 15th century wood engravings of Brabant, blossoming in the Renaissance, when it had an important part to play, for instance in the activities of the publishing house of Hieronymus Cock and the printer/publisher Christophe Plantin.

Stained glass work and tapestry-making blossomed. The painter van Orley also made models and cartoons for the stained glass windows of the St. Gudule Cathedral and the *Chasses Maximiliennes* series of tapestries. In the field of sculpture, the spirit of the Renaissance is to be found above all in the work of Jan Mone, sculptor to Charles V, and Jacques du Broeucq.

At the end of the 16th century, which was a turbulent era of political and religious problems, the artistic world was also a maelstrom of different movements and styles, particularly under the reign of Philip II. During the next century, after the Twelve Years' Truce, Antwerp flourished once again under the rule of Archduke and duchess Albert and Isabella, after a period of decline.

This period, that of the Baroque, is personified by Pieter Paul Rubens, who was moulded by the Flemish Romanism of his masters and his own eight years in Italy. His grandiose oeuvre showed a masterly skill with colour, composition

Belgian Surrealism has its own very distinctive character. One of the best known Belgian Surrealists is Paul Delvaux (b. 1897).

Vogels, James Ensor, Fernand Khnopff and Theo van Rysselberghe, but also canvases by foreign innovators like Monet, Whistler, Van Gogh, Gauguin, Lautrec, Redon etc. This was continued by the Libre Esthétique right up to 1914, and was the breeding ground of art, literature and music, where later symbolism, neo-impressionism, expressionism and all the other new movements of the 20th century were born. James Ensor is perhaps the most important of them all. After 1887, he developed into the boldest innovator of his time. Before Van Gogh, he was already using colour in a deliberately non-realistic manner, introducing a revolutionary technique and a visionary style combining the realistic with the imaginary. Thus the tradition of Bosch and Bruegel lives on.

In the field of decorative art, Art Nouveau reached new heights in Belgium with the work of the architects Victor Horta, Henri van de Velde and Paul Hankar.

All the 20th century movements show their connections with two main streams: Expressionism, a consequence of Realism, and Surrealism, which developed from a visionary approach. As regards colour, Rik Wouters, who is not very well-known outside Belgium, became a master of the Brabant style of Fauvism, a style also used by Fernand Schirren, Charles Dehoy and Willem Paerels, who all experimented with light and colour effects. Leon Spillaert is somewhere on the dividing line between formal expression and Surrealism.

in abstract art, and overshadow the exceptional achievements of the Surrealists. Nevertheless, Belgium can be proud of its great abstract artists like Victor Servranckx, who was feted everywhere by the international avantgarde, and Jozef Peeters and Pierre-Louis Flouquet. In the Surrealist movement, René Magritte was perhaps the most important figure from 1926 onwards. Magritte's art created deliberate confusion by the disconcerting juxtaposition of otherwise familiar objects, and the compelling poetic force of his work has changed our perception of many things. Another surrealist, Paul Delvaux, has also enriched the modern world of the imagination through his obsessive landscapes and recurring motifs: temples, women, trains and skeletons. The Surrealist movement, which included many more artists who deserve mention, was mainly French-speaking, and can be seen as the counterpart of the Flemish expressionist movement. Once again, Belgium appears as the crossroads of different forms of sensibility.

Just after the Second World War, a group of artists exploring the world of form and colour joined together as 'La Jeune Peinture Belge' in Brussels: Gaston Bertrand, Louis Van Lint, Anne Bonnet, Marc Mendelson, Antoine Mortier, Lismonde, Jan Cox and Jo Delahaut. One group focused on geometric structure, and another on lyrical abstraction. The art of this period was exposed to all kinds of influences, from North and South America and the Far East. This led to a colourful variety of art movements including Kinetic art, Pop art, Hyperrealism, Conceptual art and the new figurative art, all of which are proof of the continuing desire to change and develop further beyond abstract art. Belgium was also affected by this unprecedented urge to experi-

ment, this feverish activity which often resulted in the merely academic. But without it, certain trends and the personal development of great artists like Raoul Ubac, Octaaf Landuyt, Bram Bogaert, Pol Mara, Roger Raveel, Roger Somville, Marcel Broodthaers, Panamarenko etc. would not have been possible. The Cobra movement (named after the first letters of Copenhagen, Brussels and Amsterdam) was initiated in 1948 by the Belgian Christian Dotremont, and one of the leading figures was Pierre Alechinsky.

After the masterly engravings of James Ensor, a new and fruitful period dawned in this branch of art. There were the wood engravings of Frans Masereel and the work of Gustave Marchoul and René Mels, who formed the Cap d'Encre group in the sixties. Poster art, which was very much in demand in 1900, enjoyed new popularity, and in the wake of Hergé, strip cartoon art became more and more diverse.

The power and richness of the sculpture of the age is outstanding. In addition to the symbolic universe of George Minne and the startling innovations of Rik Wouters in his *Mad Dancer,* there are a wide range of artists including George Grard, Charles Leplae, Pierre Caille, Willy Anthoons, Pol Bury, Jacques Moeschal, Roel d'Haese, Olivier Strebelle and André Willequet.

Soon after the Second World War there was a new renaissance in tapestry-making, particularly in Tournai, while in Brussels, Flanders and Wallonia there was a revival of ceramic work.

This summary is proof, if proof is needed, that Belgium was and still is rich in top-level creative talent. Her artistic heritage can be seen in the museums, churches and town halls of the land, and in famous museums all over the world.

Around 1905, the Flemish expressionist school of St.-Martens-Latem emerged, with artists like Gustaaf van de Woestyne, George Minne and Valerius de Sadeleer. The second St.-Martens-Latem group, with Constant Permeke, Gust de Smet and Frits van den Berghe also inspired a remarkably creative movement. To a certain extent, these Latem artists, and Jan Brusselmans, tended to eclipse the first experiments

DUTCH LITERATURE

JOHAN FLEERACKERS

The Dutch language developed from various Germanic dialects between the 8th and 12th centuries, gradually building up a common currency of idiom and usage throughout the territory of the old Low Countries: the Netherlands of today plus the Flemish provinces of Belgium. As we have seen earlier, the language frontier between the Germanic and the Romance language areas has remained remarkably stable since the early Middle Ages. In Belgium, this invisible frontier runs from East to West.

The first flowering of the Dutch language and literature in the late Middle Ages, its decline in the 17th century and revival in the 19th century, were all linked to the vicissitudes of political life in the Low Countries. Up to the end of the 16th century, the centre of gravity lay in Flanders, and the language was consequently referred to as *Flemish*. After the separation of the northern and the southern provinces in 1648, the emphasis shifted to Holland, and intellectual life dried up in Flanders. However, with Belgian Independence in 1830, Dutch literature came to life again, and in the space of half a century, the Flemish language and intellectual life in general evolved at a breakneck pace to catch up with the last couple of centuries.

The political split between the Northern and Southern Netherlands did slow down the development of a unified form of spoken and written Dutch, certainly in comparison with English and French, but the underlying unity of the language spoken in Flanders and Holland was never in doubt. Throughout their fluctuating fortunes over the ages, both areas remained members of the same cultural and linguistic family. The Southern Netherlands in fact had a considerable influence on Dutch literature. Up to the

Hugo Claus is perhaps the most famous Flemish writer (b. 1929). In 1986 he was awarded the Prijs der Nederlandse Letteren, which is the most important literary award in Flanders and the Netherlands.

end of the 16th century, Flanders was the nerve centre of the Dutch-speaking literary world. During the revival in the 19th century, Flemish literature took on a more specifically Flemish character under the influence of the Flemish Emancipation Movement.

From the early Middle Ages, Dutch literature followed the great European literary movements. In a period when the art of writing was regarded as no more than a simple craft of monks and clerks, the academic development of the Dutch language of the people still kept pace with the evolution of the highly-skilled craftsmen of the plastic arts.

Lyricism and mysticism were the most important sources of inspiration. Historical and encyclopaedic subjects were presented at great length in verse. Hendrik van Veldeke (Limburg, before 1200) is the first well-known writer, and Jacob van Maerlandt (1225-c. 1295) the most famous of this period. Van Maerlandt was probably born in Damme near Bruges and was a didactic poet. He campaigned energetically for literature in the vernacular i.e. Middle Dutch ('Diets' or 'the language of the people', the oldest name for the Dutch language), rather than Latin or the Walloon or Romance dialects. He was honoured as the *'Father of Dutch poetry'* by his followers.

Religious mysticism occupies a very special place in early Dutch literature with the work of the poetess Hadewych (1200-c. 1260) — centuries before women's lib — and Jan van Ruusbroec (1294-1381) in Brussels. His work was translated into Latin and was widely known abroad even in his own lifetime. Ruusbroec can certainly be regarded as the first Dutch writer of European standing. Two long narrative poems of the 13th and 14th centuries are masterpieces: the moral fable

'Beatrice' and the animal epic 'Reynard the Fox', both familiar subjects in European literature. They give an interesting insight into the two poles of medieval Flemish thought: simple religious faith and the most down-to-earth and even cynical view of life here below.

The 15th century ushered in a period of formalism, with strict metres and artificial themes, but thanks to the 'Chambers of Rhetoric', Dutch literature and poetry was taken to all corners of the Dutch-speaking world, and performed in even the smallest towns and regions. Drama in particular was a popular form of folk art. Most performances were mystery plays, miracle plays or chivalric dramas, the theatrical form of the 'chanson de gèste'.

The 16th century was dominated by religious antagonism and religious wars. In the fight against the Reformation, Anna Bijns of Antwerp (1493-1575) took the lead in the defence of the Roman Catholic faith. If she had lived in our age, she would have been writing fiery leaders in the daily papers. Her opponent was Marnix van Sint Aldegonde (1540-98), Councillor of William of Orange, who fulminated against the official Church in his diatribe: *'Beehive of the Roman Church'*. The author also wrote a French version, which won European renown for both the author and his book.

In 1574, the famous printer-publisher of French origin, Christoffel Plantijn, published the first 'Dictionarium' compiled by Cornelius Kiliaan, giving a scientific definition of the words then in use in the Dutch language area.

In the 17th and 18th centuries, the flourishing Dutch literature in Flanders was forced into the background. No more writers of any substance emerged. Dutch gradually lost its natural po-

sition in political and social life, and under the Austrian rule, the Netherlands were governed in French from Vienna and Brussels. After 1648, the provinces of the Northern Netherlands took the lead. Dutch became the language of a rich nation involved in world politics and founding trade centres in many continents. In Amsterdam, the greatest Dutch poet was at work: Joost van den Vondel, whose parents had emigrated from Antwerp...

The reveille of the Dutch language in Flanders at the beginning of the 19th century was influenced by the concept of the nation based on a national language, an idea gaining currency all over Europe at this time. During the period of the United Kingdom (1815-30), William I honoured this principle by reinstating Dutch as the only official administrative language of Belgium, but with the Belgian revolution, French once again became the only official language. The Flemish Movement, which emerged as a reaction to the subordination of the Dutch language, found unexpected and passionate support from a remarkable literary revival. Two authors with widely differing styles had a determining influence here. Hendrik Conscience (1812-83), son of a French soldier who had settled in Flanders, wrote tales for the people, most of whom could hardly read. His influence on the spiritual awakening of the Flemish people was vast. His most famous work is 'the Lion of Flanders', a romantic epic evoking the glorious victory of medieval Flanders, successfully wresting a hard-won freedom from the hands of the French overlord. The parallel with the repression of the Dutch language in Belgium in their own time was obvious, and the message got over to the ordinary people too. About 1860, the voice of a truly inspired poet began to be heard: Guido Gezelle

(1830-99). For the first time since the Middle Ages, an original poetic idiom was being created in the Southern Netherlands. Like Conscience, Gezelle's importance was not only literary but also didactic: as an amateur philologist and lexicographer of Flemish idiom he helped to build up the linguistic self-respect of a repressed people.

Other writers played a part in the revival of cultural awareness through their literary works and essays. The literary movement 'Van Nu en Straks' (of today and tomorrow) tried, under the leadership of Professor August Vermeylen (1872-1945) of Ghent University, to get South Netherlands literature back into the mainstream of European intellectual life. The most important representatives of this movement were Stijn Streuvels (1871-1969), Karel van de Woestijne (1878-1929) and Herman Teirlinck (1883-1967). Apart from these literary realists, there were writers who had always found their inspiration in a more romantic view of Flemish life. 'Pallieter' brought international fame for Felix Timmermans (1866-1947), especially in Germany. Ernest Claes (1885-1968) portrayed the life of the Flemish people, and his first book 'De Witte' (The blond boy) was reprinted more than a hundred times. After the First World War, a European dimension emerged clearly in Flemish literature, both prose and poetry, with Gerard Walschap (b. 1898) and Marnix Gijsen (1899-1982) as the most outstanding innovators. Among the writers of today, Hugo Claus (b. 1929) is undoubtedly the most brilliant prose writer and poet.

With Claus, Flemish literature is once again completely in tune with literature in the Netherlands. Since the 1950s, the Grand Prize for Dutch Literature is awarded every three years by the Belgian and Dutch heads of state to the

PHILIPPE ROBERTS-JONES

most meritorious North or South Netherlands author. In 1986, this prize was awarded to Hugo Claus.

It was not until the second half of the 19th century that a revival of Flemish drama could be discerned, though it was still somewhat overshadowed by the 'big brother' of French drama, which had become well-entrenched in Flanders since the 18th century. New theatres were built in the important towns, and Flemish theatre groups were subsidised by the government. In the twenties, 'Het Vlaamse Volkstoneel' (the Flemish People's Theatre) won great popularity, even outside Flanders. Since then, theatrical productions in Flanders have been organized professionally, and there is intensive cooperation and cross-fertilisation between Flanders and the Netherlands.

The new renaissance of Dutch literature in Belgium is proof of the fact that, after its almost fatal decline, the Dutch language and culture is once again regarded as a proud and priceless heritage by the nation. The official recognition of Dutch in the Belgian constitution as one of the national languages is further confirmation of its status today. With 20 million Dutch speakers in Belgium and the Netherlands united in a *Taalunie* (language union), Dutch is also one of the official languages of the European Economic Community. Throughout Flanders and in the capital Brussels, it is an administrative and cultural medium, and a language of literature and intellectual life.

Although Belgium is divided by a natural language frontier into two almost equal geographical segments characterised from the beginning by their own separate languages — Southern Dutch in the North and Belgo-Romance in the South — this division has not always been equally rigorous in the field of literature. Belgium is a country where cultures meet and mingle, enriching each other in the process. Its French literature owes much of its specific character to this.

Shortly after 1200, the first writings in the French language emerged: Romanic deeds in Tournai, Kortrijk and Mons, lyrical works in Liège, Hainault and Brabant, the chantefable *Aucassin et Nicolette* and the writings of Adenet le Roi. The foundation and expansion of the Burgundian state had a favourable effect on intellectual and artistic life in the Belgian provinces and its Latin, Flemish and French literature. In the latter field, Jean Froissart is a well-known figure as the author of the chronicles which he collected throughout Europe. Two works by Jean d'Outremeuse are known: *La Myreur des Histors* (a legendary story) and *La Geste de Liège* (a romantic epic). Philip the Good and Charles the Bold inspired Georges Chastellain, who was known in his time as 'The pearl and the star of the chroniclers', and Philippe de Commynes, who can be regarded either as French or Belgian. The tradition of court chroniclers was continued at the court of Mechelen under Margaret of Austria, in the person of Jean Lemaire de Belges, one of the last and the best of the 'rhetoricians'.

During the next centuries, the Belgian provinces had little to offer in the field of literature, certainly in comparison with the achievements of Bruegel's and Rubens' centuries in the visual arts. There seemed to be a lack of intellectu-

al curiosity at the time, which Maria Theresa and the Austrian régime tried to stimulate by setting up a 'Société littéraire' in Brussels in 1769, transforming it three years later into the 'Académie impériale et royale des Sciences et Belles-Lettres'. But there was one independent figure: the Prince de Ligne. He was a soldier, diplomat and writer, travelling to and fro in Europe and writing about all he saw — from the great parties of Louis XV to those of Catherine II, and everything from Potsdam to Vienna. His writings were mainly in the form of portraits, letters and memoirs.

Nineteenth century Belgium saw only a late Romantic movement and some minor poets like André van Hasselt and Theodore Weustenraad, in spite of the enthusiastic reaction to the Independence of Belgium in 1830 and examples from France. It is interesting to note that, as with painting, it is through the birth of Realism that a characteristic Belgian trent began to emerge in French literature. In Brussels, in 1856, Charles de Coster and the painter Félicien Rops founded the revue *Uylenspiegel, Journal des ébats artistiques et littéraires*. This was the revue in which de Coster published his first stories, heralding his famous *Légende d'Ulenspiegel*, a universal epic in praise of liberty.

What has been called the renaissance of Belgian literature in 1880 coincides with the foundation a year later of Max Waller's *La Jeune Belgique*, a movement and a revue which began by propagating a combination of naturalism and art for art's sake. Participants included Georges Eekhoud, Georges Rodenbach, Emile Verhaeren, Jules Destrée and Camille Lemonnier. The novels of the latter like *Un Mâle* and *Happe-chair* embody the principles of the naturalist movement, which was continued by Eekhoud, Demolder et al.

But it is in the Symbolist movement that Belgium's contribution to literature is the greatest: *Bruges-la-morte* by Rodenbach, Albert Mockel and his revue *La Wallonie*, and above all in poetry, with Charles van Lerberghe and his *Entrevisions*, the intense lyricism of Emile Verhaeren, Maurice Maeterlinck and his *Serres Chaudes* and *Pelléas et Mélisande*, Nobel Prize winner for literature in 1911, and finally, Max Elskamp with his hidden depths under a simple exterior. And many others could be mentioned, all of whom have made a contribution to this universal body of literature.

The literature of the 20th century continues in the same direction, showing a close affinity with the visual arts and the 'Les Vingt' group and Art Nouveau, with figures like Fernand Khnopff, James Ensor, Victor Horta and Henri van de Velde. Immediately after the First World War, Dadaism was present in the work of Clément Pansaers and the revue *Ça Ira* edited by Paul Neuhuys. Belgium's contribution to Surrealism was substantial, both in Brussels and in Hainault, thanks to people like Paul Nougé, Marcel Lecomte, E.L.T. Mesens, Louis Scutenaire, Achille Chavée, right through to Christian Dotremont, without forgetting the greatest visual Surrealist of them all: René Magritte. All these writers maintained their individuality within the movement of their time, which has yielded a rich diversity of art.

In 1920 the 'Académie Royale de Langue et de Littérature françaises' was founded, and revues like 7 *Arts* and the *Disque Vert* were created. Between 1920-50, the work of poets like Jean de Boschère, Odilon-Jean Périer, Norge, Marcel Thiry, Robert Goffin and Henri Michaux, who were closely linked with French poetry, was gaining acclaim. The more prominent prose writers in-

The novelist George Simenon (b. 1903), a native of Wallonia, is known all over the world.

cluded André Baillon, Franz Hellens, Marie Gevers, Charles Plisnier (who won the Prix Goncourt in 1937), Albert Ayguesparse, Georges Simenon ('the greatest novelist of them all' according to André Gide), Suzanne Lilar etc., while the names of Fernand Crommelynck, Michel de Ghelderode and Paul Willems command respect as playwrights. All these people have risen above the merely regional, and then we have not even mentioned the historians and philologists — Henri Pirenne, Hen-

ri Grégoire, Charles Moeller, Georges Poulet, Carlo Bronne etc.

Contemporary art need not fear comparison with the past. The vitality of poetry, for example, emerges clearly from the International poetry biennials inaugurated in 1951, the International centre for the study of poetry and the many poetry journals, including the *Journal des Poètes,* founded by Pierre Louis Flouquet in 1936, *Marginales, Phantomas, L'Arbre à Paroles* etc.

Prose writing is highly diverse, with the fantastic world of writers following in the footsteps of Jean Ray at one end of the scale, and the realism of writers like Dominique Rolin at the other. The lure of the Rive Gauche may be great — Dominique Rolin has been living in Paris since 1946, Félicien Marceau and Marguerite Yourcenar are members of the Académie Française and Françoise Mallet-Joris has a seat in the Académie Goncourt — but there are many others who have resisted the temptation. And

everyone in France and French-speaking Belgium alike knows Joseph Hanse and his *Dictionnaire des Difficultés du Français Moderne* and Maurice Grevisse's French grammar *Le Bon Usage* — two writers born this side of Quiévrain.

MUSIC

JOHAN FLEERACKERS

Belgian museums are anything but sterile exhibition halls. Sometimes they are a good place to... make music.

Throughout medieval Europe, the influence of liturgical life on the development of music was of fundamental importance. There are very early records of musical activity in Liège, but many early medieval sources have been lost. The 15th century heralded the beginning of an exceptionally important period in the development of musical culture in Europe. The fundamental renewal of musical composition at the time can be attributed to composers from the old Dutch provinces. The 18th century German musical historian Nikolous Forkel insisted that it was not the Italians but the Low Countries who were the real founders of European music. A very flattering opinion, and just as with our fame as a nation of painters, a view which demands some explanation. Many composers were from the Dutch-speaking regions, but other masters like Guillaume Dufay (1400-74), Gillis Binchois (1400-60) and Josquin des Près (1440-1521) came from French-speaking provinces. Consequently, Francophone art historians tend to refer to the 'Franco-German school' or the Burgundian school. But be that as it may, from the 15th century on, the Low Countries were the centre of creative innovation in music. The polyphonic technique was developed there, and later adopted all over Europe. The new musical style is attributed to Jacob Obrecht (1450-1505) and Johannes Ockegem (c. 1430-95), and reached unequalled heights in the work of Josquin des Près. Luther said of him: *'Musicians do the best they can with the notes, but Josquin does exactly what he wants with them'*.

The sudden emergence of these brilliant musical reformers is still an intriguing phenomenon today. It was undoubtedly connected with the high level of culture and wealth for which the late medieval Flemish towns in particular were famous. These musicians were contemporaries and artistic brothers-in-arms of other brilliant artists like the van Eyck brothers, Dirk Bouts, Hans Memling, Rogier van der Weyden. This was also the period when the large towns looked like one great building site, where buildings of monumental proportions were constructed with mathematical precision. The literature of the day had also reached a high intellectual level. Music was one of the four universal arts, and it was predictable that in a society that had reached such heights of achievement, music should strive towards perfection and innovation. These polyphonists were much-sought-after and well-paid assistants at almost every court in Europe. In Italy in particular, they took up posts as capellmeister, like Adriaen Willaert (c. 1480-1562) in Venice, and exerted a seminal influence on the development of Italian Renaissance music. In the 16th century, in the heyday of the Dutch school in Italy, two more stars appeared in the firmament: Filip de Monte from Mechelen (1521-1602) and Orlandus Lassus from Hainault (1531-94), who left more than two thousand compositions after his death, and whom Einstein called a *universal genius*.

The fluctuating political regimes of the 17th and 18th centuries entailed a decline of artistic life on many levels, although important artists were still active in the visual arts and architecture. Music could only flourish under the wing of the Church and the secular courts, being by definition a capital-intensive activity requiring a high investment in players. In 17th and 18th century Belgium, there were only two courts: that of the Prince-bishopric of Liège and the Hapsburg court in Brussels, though a few large churches could still command a degree of music-

al splendour. Liège in particular enjoyed a second renaissance. The nobility in Brussels commissioned work from national artists, but only about 15 composers of national standing in this period are known today. In 1700, the first opera house was built in Brussels, on the site of the old Mint.

A more important aspect of this period was the surprising development of musical instrument-making. The famous Ruckers family of Antwerp, harpsichord makers, the organ maker van Peterghem and the bell-founding family van den Gheyn, all bequeathed valuable instruments to posterity. Some of these instruments have been restored and are conserved with great care today. The 'Brussels Museum of Musical Instruments' and the 'Vleeshuis' Museum in Antwerp together house 4,000 musical instruments from every continent: the richest collection in the world. In 1846, Adolf Sax (1814-94), who was born in Dinant, built the first

saxophone, after he had first made fundamental improvements in the manufacture of brass instruments. This instrument was to play an important part in jazz music in our century.

With the advent of the French Revolution, musical life came to an abrupt halt. Nevertheless, the 19th century was a turning point. Inspired by the great musical traditions of Germany and France and under the influence of romantic nationalism, a national musical style developed in every European country. In Flanders, the Flemish emancipation movement was the greatest source of artistic inspiration. Peter Benoit (1834-1901) founded a 'Flemish School of Music' in Antwerp in 1867, and this was later to become the 'Royal Flemish Academy of Music'. But Benoit's greatest achievements were the creation of deeply impressive lyrical oratorios in exalted praise of Flanders' artistic glory and her landscape. An important factor in the development

of religious music was the foundation in 1878 of a 'Higher Institute of Church Music' by the organist and composer Jaak Lemmens. This institute, now called the 'Lemmens Institute', made a great contribution to the renaissance of organ music in Belgium, with Flor Peeters (1905-86) as one of its most eminent sons.

César Franck was born in Liège in 1822. He is the most gifted and famous Belgian composer of modern times. However, he spent all his life working in Paris, where he attracted many followers. Franck's compositions, which are of truly Latin inspiration, and those of Benoit are two different worlds which to a certain extent illustrate the differences in artistic affinities between the two communities in Belgium.
At the end of the century, the work of three outstanding violinists, Charles de Bériot of Louvain (1802-70), Henri Vieuxtemps (1820-70) and Eugène Ysaye (1858-1931) of Verviers, came to-

Belgium is not only a land of painters, but also of musicians. Many Belgian composers and musicians have won world fame.

gether to form the so-called *Belgian school of violin music*. They were all important composers, but their most important contribution was their teaching. Composers today are influenced by the eclectic style which is typical of our times. Musical life in Brussels owes much to the late Queen Elisabeth, who was a good violinist with a great interest in music. She inspired the creation of a 'Palais des Beaux-Arts' in Brussels in the 1920s, and was also behind the creation of the famous International Eugène Ysaye Competition in 1937. After the war, the competition was renamed the Queen Elisabeth Competition. It is held in rotation for violinists, pianists, singers and composers, and has become one of the most important international competitions in the music world. It is held in the Palais des Beaux-Arts, a creation of the architect Horta.

The international 'Youth and Music' movement was also born in that same Palais des Beaux-Arts, under the leadership of Marcel Cuvelier during the war years. Today, Youth and Music organizes introductory concerts for young people in all towns in Belgium.

Orchestral activities developed relatively late in Belgium, in contrast with the flourishing world of opera, and perhaps even because of it. In accordance with the French tradition of opera handed down from the 18th century, opera houses were built in Brussels, Ghent, Liège and Verviers, where work was performed by visiting or resident troupes of varying quality and with varying success. The history of Belgian independence has close ties with opera, because the freedom aria in the opera 'La Muette de Portici' triggered the first anti-government demonstration against William I of the Netherlands in Brussels in August 1830.

The heavy investment in these opera houses held back the formation and financing of independent symphony orchestras in Belgium longer than elsewhere. The 'National Orchestra of Belgium' was set up in 1936, but it was not until the fifties that independent orchestras could be created in other towns.

Today, there are resident orchestras in Antwerp, Liège and Ghent, providing a wide range of concerts for the public. Smaller companies have specialised in ancient music, and can pride themselves on a number of virtuosi of international renown, and a great many performances on record. Musical life blossomed spectacularly in the sixties. Throughout the ages, musical culture has flourished in times of economic expansion, and this was abundantly so in the golden sixties. Art and music academies were established in many towns, and the Gemeentekrediet van België initiated an annual national music competition for the young people studying at these academies. But the most impressive achievement of these years is the explosive growth of a number of music festivals. Since 1958, the *Festival of Flanders* has developed into one of the major music events in Europe. The *Festival of Wallonia* is a similar event which is held in various towns in Wallonia.

Belgium is also a country which can pride itself on the high level of its popular brass bands, and there are countless amateur brass bands all over the country. Many towns have a selection of flourishing choirs too, and the German-speaking community has produced the excellent Eupener Männerquartett, which can no longer be fairly described as a quartet.

Opera, which is at the roots of musical life in Belgium, is currently enjoying a

remarkable revival. Under the stimulus of its young artistic manager, Gerard Mortier, who has been leading the National Opera since 1981, the Munt Opera house in Brussels has risen to the position of one of the most influential opera centres in the world. The two Regions have each merged their opera houses: the 'Opéra National de Wallonie — Centre lyrique de la Communauté française de Liège' and the 'Opera voor Vlaanderen' which groups

together the historical opera houses of Antwerp and Ghent.

In the field of ballet, Belgium had little to offer. Then in 1962 the *20th Century Ballet* was set up under the leadership of the French choreographer Maurice Béjart, and the troupe soon won worldwide fame, introducing a new style of choreography. Ballet had now carved out a permanent place in artistic life in Belgium. Within a short space of time,

Anne-Maria De Keersmaecker and her group 'Rosas' enjoy international renown.

successful ballet companies were also set up in Liège and Antwerp, performing both at home and abroad.

But time does not stand still here either. The international style of music attracted an enthusiastic following here among the young and the middle generation, as elsewhere in the Western world, and each new musical cult plays Pied Piper to its adoring fans. The Anglo-Saxon sound has become the new common ground of music appreciated all over the world, replacing the charismatic liturgical music of centuries past. In the field of popular music, English is the lingua franca of the communication of the emotions. The Torhout-Werchter Festival took off to become the biggest annual rock festival in Europe within the space of a few years. But so far, no Belgian groups have been able to make a real breakthrough on the international scene. A few rare talents managed to make it to the international top — but from a foreign base, like Toots Thielemans, who needed America as his stepping stone to success as a jazz guitarist and harmonica player, and the great Jacques Brel, who launched his profoundly Belgian chansons in Paris.

Text:
LUCIE SPÈDE

The people of Belgium welcome their 'Red Devils' after the World Cup in Mexico.

Ghent is a city of typically Belgian contrasts, with its thriving industry, commerce and modern sea-port side by side with the tranquil charm and dignity of architecture dating back to the 12th century.

For its 350,000 inhabitants and its many visitors, Ghent is teeming with life: flower shows, trade fairs, conferences, opera, music festivals, theatre, museums of ancient and modern art and artefacts — something for everyone. The dense road network and national and international train services make Ghent easily accessible, and the rivers and canals which run through the very heart of the city lend it a unique charm as they reflect the superb facades of the Guild Halls, the old covered markets, castles and palaces.

LIVELY LIÈGE

The river Meuse, one of the great waterways of Europe, and the fighting spirit of the people of Liège have made it one of the most important commercial and industrial centres of Belgium since the Middle Ages.

The Liège region is famous for its steelworks, blast furnaces, chemical plants and the few working collieries still surviving from the heyday of coal mining in the 19th century. Over the ages, Liège has been a leader in the manufacture of glass and arms and still is today, while the region is now also evolving towards the diversification of its metallurgical industry.

This same river Meuse makes Liège the third most important river port of Western Europe, and it is also one of the great international crossroads of road and rail networks. The city of Liège itself has conserved much of its historical heritage which dates back to the 8th century, and has created one of the largest pedestrian precincts in Europe. It is a pleasure to stroll through the various quarters of the town, ranging from exclusive elegance to cosy working class quarters, through the narrow streets of the Outre-Meuse, which inspired Georges Simenon. Or to see the many museums and parks, or mingle with the crowds at the Sunday market along the banks of the Meuse, with its vivid variety of sounds and colours and stalls piled high with everything under the sun.

ANTWERP, WHERE TRADE IS A FINE ART

Each year, 16,000 seagoing ships and some 80,000 inland shipping vessels put in at this ancient port still redolent of the Middle Ages. But its ancient fame still holds good today: it is the third most important port in the world and moreover one of the most productive. With its ultra-modern facilities and experienced personnel, the port of Antwerp can handle freight swiftly and accurately.

Its industrial estate covers more than 3,000 hectares and includes domestic and foreign enterprises, mainly in the petrochemical industry, and the metropolis itself welcomes commercial activities and tourism.

Visitors can follow in the footsteps of Antwerp's great painter Rubens and admire his work in the Cathedral or in his superb baroque studio.

Art is predominant too in the Middelheim Park where contemporary sculpture is exhibited in the open air. And the consummate art of Antwerp's cutters of precious stones has made it the world centre of the diamond trade, and Belgium the top world exporter in this field.

The people of this affluent and enterprising town enjoy the good things of life, relaxing expansively in the scores of little cafés and nightclubs, on the waters of the Scheldt in a sight-seeing boat, a yacht or on skis, or at the zoo — all attractions which draw tourists from all over the world, just as much as the works of Rubens, van Eyck and Memling, or the more recent Permeke, Pol Mara, Jos Hendrickx, Jozef Vinck and Jan Cox.

A BASTION OF BEAUTY
ON THE BANKS OF THE MEUSE

The stern fortifications around Namur still bear witness to its long history of resistance to besiegers envious of its unique strategic position on the confluence of the Meuse and the Sambre.

But today, its citadel has been transformed into an outstanding tourist attraction, besieged only by happy visitors who throng the boulevards of the old ramparts. As the capital of the County of Namur since the 10th century, it has always been an important commercial centre. The modern shops of Namur today carry on this tradition in a town which is now the administrative centre of the province of the same name.

These shops are side by side with a 13th century tower, a 14th century belfry, the ancient Butchers' Hall (1560), baroque and Gothic churches, beautiful residences dating from the 17th and 18th centuries, museums and treasures like the priceless silverwork created by Hugues d'Oignies in the 13th century.

But the crowning glory is the beauty of the seven valleys of the province which encircle the town, with their famous chateaux and abbeys and prehistoric sites.

THE VENICE OF THE NORTH

It is easy to forget that the peaceful Bruges of today was a clamourous and exceptionally prosperous world trade centre from the 14th century to the middle of the 15th century. At the time, it was the most populous, cosmopolitan town in Europe, and the most affluent. The 20th century brought the revival of its trade with the construction of the Bruges-Zeebrugge canal, and the subsequent expansion and modernisation of Zeebrugge as a dynamic sea port. But the true face of Bruges can be seen reflected in the still waters under its ancient buildings, and in the timeless charm of its narrow streets: the venerable crenellated facades, the warm colours of its rooftops, chimes ringing out from carillons in belfries and bell towers, 15th century palaces with their precious collections, the long 12th century hospital and Chapel housing masterpieces by the Flemish Primitive Hans Memling...

CHRISTIANITY ON THE MARCH

The first evangelists were active in Belgium around the 3rd century, and traces of a Christian basilica dating from the late 4th century or early 5th century can be seen near Arlon. In the course of the second wave of evangelism, Clovis, king of the Franks, was converted in Tournai, and his people followed his example. Thereafter, more and more religious edifices were erected, especially under the reign of our Christian Emperor Charlemagne. Over the ages, Christian architecture followed the general evolution in Europe and the influence of the successive foreign rulers.

The cathedrals (this is Tournai Cathedral) and churches (St. Louis in Namur and St. Jacques in Liège for instance) bear witness to the masterly skill of Belgium's builders, artisans and artists. In addition to these Roman Catholic edifices, there are also many romanesque, Gothic, baroque and modern religious buildings, as eloquent proof of the influx of people from abroad and Belgian tolerance of their religious beliefs.

STYLISH SOUVENIRS

The first covered shopping precinct in the world was created in Brussels in 1847.

Today, the very same Galeries Royales Saint-Hubert with their perfectly preserved architecture attract flocks of visitors from Belgium and abroad to their luxury boutiques, theatres, cinemas, teashops, cafés and restaurants, whatever the weather.

Lace from Bruges, Brussels, Mechelen, Ghent, Tournai... the art of lacemaking is still practised with astonishing skill and diversity. A lace souvenir is very popular among tourists, from a tiny, not-too-expensive lace butterfly to a sumptuous tablecloth or evening dress.

Other tempting items visitors love to take home include chocolates, antiques, brasses from Dinant and crystal.

BRUSSELS, CAPITAL OF EUROPE

Brussels began humbly enough, built on a marsh which has long since been filled in. But from the 14th century onwards, it has been a prosperous, active town thriving on its cloth trade, and a beautiful place with its fountains, fortresses, churches and monuments in the shelter of thick stone ramparts. Brussels became even more attractive during the next century, extending its town hall and adding a tower, and creating all kinds of embellishments to please the Dukes of Burgundy, rulers of all the principalities of Belgium. And another advantage made itself felt: Brabant was at the centre of the Low Countries, and Brussels was at the heart of Brabant. Consequently, Brussels came to be one of the court centres of the Dukes of Burgundy and their councillors, who moved from one city to another (Bruges, Lille, the Hague) according to the needs of state. In the course of the next century (as Louis Verniers explains in his 'Le Bréviaire des Belges'), Brussels became the capital of the country.

This foreshadowed the position of Brussels today, when it is indeed the economic, political and cultural crossroads of Europe, and the gateway to the main motorways, airports, railway networks and waterways of Europe, as well as the North Sea.

A cosmopolitan capital and the headquarters of the EEC, NATO and several hundred international and American companies, Brussels is a melting-pot for the cultures and the languages of the world.

Its architecture and its 'art de vivre' reflects the world, past, present and future.

A bewildering variety of entertainment, museums, restaurants, markets, sports centres and parks of all sizes make Brussels a town to enjoy as well as an important centre for the world of finance, services and business.

BREATHTAKING OR PEACEFUL

Winding rivers full of fish, their waters gliding smoothly past or raging tempestuously between the rocky banks and forests of the Ardennes, the gentle undulations of green fields where a village nestles: the landscape of Belgium is an ever-changing panorama.

TREES LIKE TOWERS...

In the Hauts Fagne and in the Ardennes — and right up to the gates of Brussels — forests reign in splendour over almost 20 % of Belgium.

This Abbey in Grimbergen has been brooding over these same fields of Brabant since the 12th century.

There are about 75 convents and monasteries all over Belgium, built over the centuries for various religious orders. Monks and nuns may not be so numerous today, but canticles can still be heard in the echoing silence.

LIFE IN THE CASTLE

Castles and manor houses can be found all over the country, hidden in the forest, at the waterside or perched on a hill. Each one is unique, and all are worth a visit...

Many of these castles present concerts and plays or open to the public to show their antique furniture and tapestries, or to mount tournaments like those held in the rugged Horst castle in Sint-Pieters-Rode.

THE LUNGS OF THE COUNTRY

Belgium grows wheat, barley, winter barley, spelt, rye, oats, maize, fodder crops, beet and hops. With almost half of the country used for agriculture, Belgium has no shortage of peaceful horizons.

FROM THE FOREST TO THE HOME

For centuries, the forests of the Ardennes have stimulated another home-grown industry: furniture-making. Paintings by the Belgian old masters, and our museums, are full of magnificent sideboards, chests and credence tables which bear eloquent witness to the wealth of their owners. This style of furniture-making is still alive today in the very popular rustic furniture from Mechelen, where furniture is also made in the style of all ages.

The skill and inventivity of furniture-makers are forever breaking new ground in the art, as with the graceful lines of Horta and Bovy, or the minimalist style of our modern Belgian designers.

Lines, colours, techniques and materials have all changed radically, but our fame stays the same.

Belgian furniture can be seen and touched at the internationally renowned Salon du Meuble which has been held in Brussels since 1933 — in itself quite an achievement.

Loving care is lavished on trees in Belgium, making them a popular product abroad: the EEC holds up their high quality as an example.

THE LANDSCAPE IS ALWAYS GREEN

The flax being cut here and the textiles made from it are important Belgian export products. Since the Middle Ages, Belgian flax workers have been processing flax by water retting, which yields longer fibres than land retting. Further processed and worked up by specialists, it makes exceptionally attractive and hard-wearing household linen and clothing.

This young lady has escaped from the herd, and out of the meadow (which is admirably free of dandelions, in the best stockbreeding tradition). She is of one of these breeds patiently bred for productivity stocks which are even exported abroad as dairy cattle, for slaughter or selective breeding.

A COUNTRY OF ORCHARDS AND GARDENS

Half of all land used for agriculture is devoted to fruit-growing, and apples alone account for one third of this. Strawberries, pears, plums and peaches benefit from a variety of microclimates and soil types in Belgium which yield distinctly superior and flavoursome fruit. Grapes in particular, which are grown under glass according to an age-old tradition, achieve a flavour and a degree of perfection rarely equalled elsewhere.

Growing flowers, 'creating' new types, picking them to weave the transitory beauty of a flower carpet, exporting 90 % of our begonias, 80 % of our azaleas and more than half our total rose production to more than 20 different countries — every year — this is an agronomic achievement which also adds to the beauty of the countryside !

FRUITFUL RESEARCH

Spearhead researchers in molecular biology and genetic engineering continue to increase agricultural output, diversifying and improving the quality of vegetables, fruit, cereals and flowers, combatting plant viruses and finding simpler and more profitable agricultural techniques. The agricultural world is eager for progress and quick to take advantage of new possibilities opened up by research.

With modern techniques, careful attention and impeccable hygiene, primary foodstuffs are processed into top quality products. Belgium's relatively modest agricultural output is mainly for domestic use and for export to our immediate neighbours: 85 % is exported to the EEC.

AN INDUSTRY AND A FEAST FOR THE EYE

North Sea fishing is a modest industry with an output of some 33,000 tonnes: enough to cover national consumption, but also a joy to watch in action, with its variegated fleet of fishing boats, from the sober trawler to smaller, brightly-coloured craft.

BLONDE OR BRUNETTE —
THEY'RE ALL DELICIOUS

Sitting down in good company with
one of the lagers or brown beers brew-
ed in Belgium — and there are 500 -
odd to choose from — is a pleasure
which never fades. Some breweries are
industrial, others artisanal, and even the
smallest receive requests from impor-
ters for supplies of their specialities.
Many customers, like Black Africa, have
gone even further, and have asked Belgium to build breweries and to train
personnel in their countries.

EDUCATION FOR ALL

From early childhood to the age of 18, every Belgian national and all children of foreign parents resident in Belgium are offered free compulsory education provided by the State. Alternatively, they are also free to opt for private education.

The education system is highly diversified, in order to develop every aptitude and vocation. From secondary school onwards, programmes are offered covering classical subjects, technical, professional and artistic training, and special schooling is also available for pupils with mental or physical handicaps.

The many international companies operating in Belgium and the members of the EEC working here have also led to the establishment of schools teaching in languages other than Dutch or French. Belgium already has nine European Schools, (the first dating from 1958), where young people from different cultures and speaking different languages are given the same education together, an experience guaranteed to promote mutual comprehension and tolerance.

Belgium's newest university has been established in a whole new custom-built town: Louvain-la-Neuve. This remarkable complex offers facilities for 18,000 students, including lecture rooms, auditoriums, shops, cafés, restaurants and accommodation, all in a delightful rural setting a few kilometres from the capital.

Louvain-la-Neuve carries on the tradition upheld by the 5 other universities and 7 university institutes of Belgium, a task first undertaken by the University of Louvain in 1425: the provision of high-level education which has attracted students from all over the world since the 15th century.

Research and robotization in harness at the Institut national des Radio-Eléments at Fleurus.

Revolutionary applications of molecular and atomic science have been developed here in the field of medicine, food preservation, hygiene etc.

The design and manufacture of sophisticated, high-performance chips has become a speciality in both Flanders and Wallonia, as a result of close cooperation between research and industry. Remarkable new processes have been developed, improving the quality of the microelements. Here we see a resin undergoing special treatment for application in electronic printed circuit boards much in demand all over the world.

NEW TECHNIQUES: NEW ART

Research goes hand-in-hand with creation. This gold pendant is set with precious stones — and a hologram. A fascinating field of technology in which Belgium enjoys a spearhead position. This piece of jewellery, the first of its kind, came into being through the joint efforts of the artist Octave Landuyt and Professor A.G. Vinckier, Director of the Laboratory of Material Science and Welding Technology of the University of Ghent.

Computers can also stimulate and increase the range of creativity. They can enable us to conjure up instantly all the thousand and one lay-out possibilities for a page of text, for example, or for packaging, printing or designing a dress...

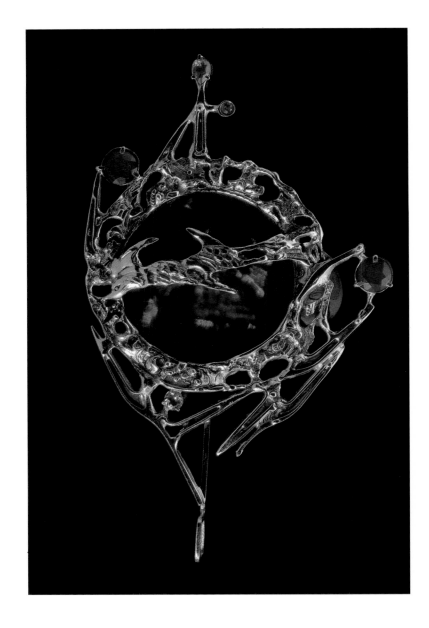

ENERGY ALL AROUND US

Seven power stations in Belgium harness nuclear energy, while others pluck energy from the wind, like these 23 wind-driven generators at the new seaport at Zeebrugge. They each have a capacity of 200 kw and are computer-controlled from a central post. As their white blades turn, they seem to be waving amicably to the old windmills enjoying a picturesque retirement. Both nuclear and wind-powered generators contribute to Belgium's substantial energy exports.

INDUSTRY ON THE MOVE

Belgium has become a specialist in the automobile sector and the largest exporter in Europe, with robots on the assembly line and a workforce to put the finishing touches to vehicles of all types. Most European automobile manufacturers have opted for assembly facilities in Belgium.

Orders pour in from all over the world for coaches, trains, trams and metros adapted to the needs of each client. Their technical performance, resilience, comfort and esthetic qualities have been tried and tested since the 1880s when Belgium played its part in the construction of the famous Paris metro and the superlative Orient Express.

SACRED FIRE

The modern descendants of the ancient smiths are ready to tackle anything. Some Belgian manufacturers specialise in products based on the most complex alloys of nonferrous metals. Perhaps this is what they mean by 'sacred fire'...

MASTERING METAL

The Belgians have mastered metal in all its manifestations while manufacturing or treating metals or even creating new alloys.

Iron and steel, brass and aluminium and a variety of alloys are exported far beyond our frontiers in the form of building reinforcements, pipelines, rails, suspension bridges for Bangkok, wrought ironwork, sheet metal, pipes, steel profiles and ingots, vehicles, industrial equipment and appliances of all kinds. Metals are among our 50 most extensively exported products.

CENTURIES OF PAINSTAKING CARE

An intimate technical and intuitive knowledge of the material, a good eye and a sure touch, experience based on a long tradition and a deep love for the trade: these are the qualities which have built up the world fame of diamonds cut in Antwerp and hunting arms manufactured in Herstal. And this renown is still growing, with diamond exports up 17.5 % between 1985 and 1986, and exports to Japan alone up 90 %.

INVENTIONS WHICH TRAVEL ALL ROUND THE WORLD AGAIN AND AGAIN

The aeronautical industry in Belgium is in robust good health, thanks to many factors, including its participation in the design and production of the Airbus project.

Cooperation between university and industry is both spectacular and effective at the Sart-Tilman industrial research park. One of its most famous establishments is Ital Space, the space department of the Institute of Astrophysics of Liège. It has successfully participated in the research and execution of large-scale European space projects like the recent Giotto space probe launched in pursuit of Halley's comet, and the Hipparcos satellite project. In addition to these European scientific activities, Ital Space also tenders for contracts with industry for projects in the field of opto-electronics and opto-informatics, and others.

This videoprojector produced by a West Flanders company has made the firm a world leader in the sector. All types of video recordings can be projected with this model, Pal, Secam or American cassettes, thus facilitating the exchange of information the whole world over. It can be used as a front or back projector, and for satellite-linked international television conferences.

SPANNING THE SCALE FROM
THE MINUTE TO THE COLOSSAL

Articles designed for the general public, professional equipment or sophisticated industrial installations: Belgium has proved its competence in the field of electronics. This is the home of the Compact Disc and CD player, widely acclaimed by music-lovers all over the world. And Belgium has also provided the concepts and the equipment used in so many digital telephone exchanges, banks, metro buildings and airport halls throughout the world, where illuminated displays and control panels are more and more often labelled 'Made in Belgium'.

Since the beginning of the industrial era, Belgian companies have specialised in the manufacture of mechanical and electrical machines. Today, this has expanded to include the creation of systems based on telemetry and electronics, setting up fully-automated rolling mills and cement works for instance, and a fully-automated control system for urban transport, equipment for satellites and rockets etc... Nevertheless, vast steam turbines and gigantic generators still figure prominently in export orderbooks.

THE BOUNDLESS VISTAS OF CHEMISTRY

Research is also one of the pillars of our chemical industry, and has been since the beginning in 1863. Today, a staff of 2,800 is busy developing the products of the future at the Solvay Research Centre in Brussels and in its laboratories.

The activities of the Solvay Group include chemistry and biochemistry, synthetic products and their applications, and pharmaceutical products for human and animal use. The Group has establishments in 31 countries, including 18 in Europe, and employs more than 44,000 people.

IN SEARCH OF HEALTH

The largest pharmaceutical research laboratory in the world is in Belgium. The quality of our scientists and their equipment have enabled them to achieve remarkable successes, like the development of a vaccine against Hepatitis-B by means of genetic engineering. This new Belgian vaccine is of constant quality and can be obtained without recourse to donors. It is now being used to combat a virus which was responsible for 2 million deaths every year.

THE WORLD'S NO. 1 EXPORTER OF CARPETS

Back in the Middle Ages, Belgian craftsmen saw their creations sent out from Tournai, Kortrijk, Oudenaarde and Brussels to castles and country houses in France, Germany and Holland. Who would have dreamed then that today, Belgian carpets of all types and styles

would be in demand as far afield as Arabia? Or that one carpet-owner out of every three in Europe today owns a carpet made in Belgium?

FASHION WITH A FOLLOWING

Natural fibres, synthetic fibres, mixed fibres — being worked here by one of Belgium's 850,000 immigrants — textiles rank fifth in the export products league table in Belgium.

A new generation of fashion designers has whipped these textiles up into delicious new concoctions, proclaiming proudly that 'Fashion starts in Belgium'. A fashion which is coolly classical or wildly audacious, with imaginatively designed leatherwear and furs.

FROM OUR FAMOUS DENIM TO TEXTILES FOR CIVIL ENGINEERING

Denim, that famous blue thread which is made up into hard-wearing jeans, is turned out by the kilometre from Belgium's hypermodern weaving mills, making Belgium the largest producer of denim in the world.

An even more hard-wearing type of textile, which, however, is intended for quite different applications, are the new geotextiles. When manufactured as a net, this material is strong enough to contain firmly the huge blocks of the jetty of the port of Zeebrugge. It is also used to support and retain the earthworks when a canal is being dug.

THE TECHNOLOGY OF THE FUTURE

This model company, which specialises in the manufacture of custom-built electronic chips, is a good example of the competence with which many small businesses in Belgium adapt to radical changes in concepts, markets and specific requests from clients.

THE TRANSMISSION OF THOUGHTS AND INFORMATION

We have come a long way since 1473, when Thierry Maertens of Aalst introduced the technique of printing with movable letters into the Netherlands.

Today, Belgium is teeming with top-quality printers with high-performance equipment at their disposal.
Art books with fine quality reproductions, brightly-coloured strip cartoons, temptingly illustrated cookery books, novels, magazines, newspa-

pers, publicity material: the printing presses have plenty to do, and the International Book Fair in Brussels attracts a dense throng of cosmopolitan visitors every year.

Today, the written word is supported more and more by verbal and visual communication. Belgium has developed a telecommunications network linking it up with the world, mainly by satellite.

Belgium's central location and good infrastructures, together with its organizational flair, made it the ideal choice for the headquarters of Eurovision.

ANTWERP, GHENT, ZEEBRUGGE: HIGHLY PROFITABLE PORTS

These three ports give the area the highest concentration of port facilities in the world, backed up by the inland ports of Brussels and Liège. Antwerp, Ghent and Zeebrugge are renowned for their state-of-the-art port installations, their staff's high degree of professionalism and the rarity of disruption through industrial action.

Antwerp, Belgium's largest port and the third largest in the world, is an important transit port for traffic between Europe, Africa and the Middle East. An average of 52 million tonnes of bulk goods passes through Antwerp every year, plus 32 million tonnes of mixed cargo. Ghent specialises in rapid and efficient handling of bulk cargoes. Europe has only four seaports which are really deep: Zeebrugge is one of them, and it is considered to be one of the best-equipped on the Continent. With its excellent infrastructure, it is eminently suitable as an energy terminal, and liquid natural gas is stored here.

A COMMUNICATIONS NETWORK FOR MERCHANDISE AND MAN

The ports of Belgium are linked by a dense network of roads, motorways, fast railway lines and large shipping canals, together comprising an industrial and commercial complex on a far larger scale than one might expect from Belgium's short coastline.
This network serves a hinterland stretching far beyond our national frontiers and comprising the whole of industrial Europe.

BRUCARGO:
EUROPE'S ONLY CARGO TOWN

Brucargo is the first airport for freight in the world to have been designed from the outset to provide a full range of efficient, fast and reliable cargo handling services.

Here you will find all the airlines, customs brokers, forwarding agents, handling companies, customs, the PTT and other services, all on one site.

Brucargo's location only two minutes away from the biggest intersection in Europe giving immediate access to the European motorway network means that freight can be dispatched with a minimum of delay. And post can be forwarded in record time, because more and more private courier services are using Brucargo and Brussels National Airport as the pivot of their express services.

Despite having so much to offer, it is still one of the cheapest airports for freight in Europe.

THE AIRPORT AT THE HEART OF EUROPE: BRUSSELS NATIONAL

Only 12 km from the centre of the Belgian capital, the international airport of Brussels welcomes some 6 million passengers every year, and serves more than 100 destinations.

Like the rest of Belgium, the airport combines efficiency with a human face: computers have made it easier to chart the movements of the aircraft and arrivals and departures, and have accelerated the completion of registration formalities, embarkation and control, but have not dehumanized the place. You can stroll around and take your choice of the bars, cafés and restaurants, select a tax-free souvenir in one of the attractive boutiques or in the self-service shop, relax in one of the waiting rooms or rest areas, or make use of the many services available including foreign exchange, postal and telegraphic services, telephones, banks, tourist information, chapels, left-luggage lockers, free hotel reservation etc.

Sabena's aircraft and those of many other foreign airlines are pampered planes: the availability of highly-qualified local technical staff and the excellent facilities of Sabena and Teamco in particular have prompted airlines from all over the world to choose the national airport of Brussels-Zaventem for the maintenance of their aircraft.

Sabena's modern fleet of planes serves 72 destinations in 49 different countries, transporting about 2 million passengers and 100 million kg. of merchandise every year.

In 1835, the first train on the European continent started up a service linking Brussels and Mechelen. Since then, a dense railway network has been built up all over the country, offering passengers a punctual service in comfortable trains, the latest of which sport brilliant colours!

HOTELS FOR EVERYONE

Permanent exhibitions, temporary museums, technical congresses, international conferences and trade fairs, symposiums and seminars: an endless stream of meetings in the larger towns of Belgium. And an endless stream of visitors here for business or for pleasure. More than two thousand hotels,

motels and guesthouses are here to accommodate them, totalling almost 90,000 beds, plus about 4,000,000 offered by more modest establishments, including camping sites.

Belgians are not ashamed of their love of good food, be it a Pantagruelian pot of stew for a people's festival in Bruges or the refined delicacy of the French cuisine. It's all here to be enjoyed, for us and for our visitors.

THE CHANGING SPECTACLE OF THE STREETS

Yes, umbrellas grow like mushrooms in the streets of Belgium! The climate is temperate, with average temperatures ranging between 2.6°C in January and 17.1°C in July. A flurry of snow, a flash of sun, a gentle climate where showers make the soil more fertile — and put a broad grin on the face of the raincoat sellers!

On certain days or evenings, the streets and squares come to life with tableaux vivant and the characters of days gone by.

Here, in the Ommegang in Brussels, we have Charles V, ruler of the Holy Roman Empire, once again in his favourite capital, surrounded by the local nobility. They are entertained by stilt-walkers, jugglers and acrobats wearing the same colourful costumes as their predecessors in ages past. The setting is superb: the Grand Place in Brussels.

BRUGES:
A PEACEFUL BEGUINE CONVENT...

'A tranquil peace within the walls
As evening bells call sweetly,
With folded hands and downcast eyes,
Like swans on peaceful waters,
The faithful flock together.'

With this shining symbol of the World Exhibition in 1958, Belgium reaffirmed its faith in progress, prosperity and opening its doors to the world.

On the plateau of Mont-Saint-Jean, just outside Brussels, a hillock and a lion dominate the famous battlefield of Waterloo, almost unchanged since 18 June 1815, when the joint forces of Europe routed the Napoleonic army and captured the Emperor of France.

WHERE WAR HAS PASSED OVER

Despite its neutrality, Belgium was ravaged during the two great wars of the 20th century.
Here, in the cemetry of Ypres, soldiers of many nations lie side by side in tragic brotherhood.

DEFENCE

The total strength of the Belgian Army is about 97,000, two-thirds of whom are professional soldiers, both men and women. They are duly trained in one of the three forces: land, sea or air. This army makes a substantial contribution to NATO, as these pupils of the Ecole Militaire demonstrate.

THE PALAIS DE JUSTICE: A MAGISTERIAL EDIFICE

Designed between 1866 and 1883 by the Belgian architect J. Poelaert in the 'eclectic' style, the imposing building dominates Brussels with its huge dome, its Babylonian colonnades and enormous cornice a kilometre long. Justice reigns with impartiality in all the

countless chambers linked by vast halls and echoing staircases. The grandiose dimensions of this edifice reflected both the new importance of the Belgian nation and the respect due to the abso-lute independence of the magistrature.

A ROUND CHAMBER FOR
THE DEPUTIES

As a parliamentary democracy and a
hereditary monarchy, Belgium respects
the separation of power as laid down in
the Constitution of 1831.
Legislative power is exercised by Parliament and the King. Parliament is composed of the Chamber of Representa-

tives (or Deputies) and the Senate: their
members are elected by the people.
Executive power is bestowed by the
King and the Ministers he has appointed
to govern.
Judicial power is exercised independently by the courts and tribunals, in the
name of the King, who has the right of
granting pardon.

When their country was created in 1830, the people of Belgium opted for a constitutional, parliamentary and hereditary monarchy. They have remained faithful to this choice, which has proved to be their best guarantee of democratic liberty.

As a symbol of the cohesion and unity of the nation, the Monarchy in Belgium exercises a higher function of authority. It is the guardian of national independence, territorial unity, the common heritage and the rights and liberties of the citizens, and as such, represents an element of continuity and an impartial view.

The tasks of the Monarchy with its political aspects and symbolic and representative roles are many and varied. The King is involved in one way or another in the exercise of the legislative, executive and judiciary powers, commands the armed forces, awards military orders and concludes peace, alliance and trade treaties.

He plays a part in public life through speeches dealing mainly with domestic or foreign politics or subjects of general interest, particularly in the field of economics and intellectual and moral questions.

Further, the King can also exert a certain influence on political life in general, maintain contacts with political leaders and the opposition, underline his view of the interests of the nation, and formulate warnings when necessary.

As the representative of the nation, the King and Queen carry out visits all over Belgium as well as abroad. Courtesy visits, friendship visits, marking a social, cultural or economic interest in individuals, institutions or countries: a multitude of such visits are packed into the royal diary throughout the monarch's lifetime.

King Baudouin, Queen Fabiola and the other members of the royal family incarnate the image of Belgium in the world, performing this role with a truly Belgian cordiality and effectiveness.

THE TOWN HALL OF LOUVAIN
WITHIN THESE WALLS, URBAN
INDEPENDENCE FLOURISHED

The autonomy of our towns was one of the proudest achievements of our fore-fathers, who expressed this pride flamboyantly, and often in stone. Towns and villages jealously defended this tradition.

Between the 10th and the 14th century, the independent spirit of the Belgians led them to dare to gradually impose the quasi-autonomy of their rich cities on their rulers.

Once authorized by charters to run their own administration, organize their own defence and levy their own taxes, the communes erected town halls, bell towers, perrons and fortified town walls — all proud outward signs of what was in effect their independence. By thus establishing the respective rights and duties of the nobility and the communes, joint management of the country and the protection of the citizens, regions like Liège and Flanders, for example, arrived at certain positions several centuries earlier than the French Revolution.

THE HEADQUARTERS OF HIGH FINANCE AND THE ECONOMY

Brussels is the 7th largest financial market in the world and the 4th largest in Europe. Many foreign banks are well-represented in the major towns of Belgium, and Belgian banks have branches even in the villages. The switch to computers in the banking world was achieved here in record time.

A VETERAN OF INDUSTRIAL
ARCHEOLOGY

This hydraulic ship-lift built in the last
century is one of the last in Europe, and
it still works perfectly.

MASTERPIECES FOR A PRIVATE MANSION

Designed for Armand Solvay, this residence is one of the major creations of a great artist: the architect Horta, who was one of the leading figures in Brussels in the artistic and architectural revolution of Art Nouveau.

Horta's fame and his style were a powerful influence as far afield as America and Japan, drawing lovers of beauty to Brussels. There are still dozens of examples of Horta's architecture in our capital, built with robust materials and graceful style. Every aspect of his art can be admired here, all embodying what he himself described as 'le délicat superflu qui s'ajoute a la rude nécessité'.

EMINENTLY ROYAL GLASSHOUSES

It took nine years to build them (1870-1879), on the basis of a metal framework designed by Balat, who numbered Horta among his pupils.

The glasshouses of Laeken were built at the request of King Léopold II and from every point of view, they are truly fit for a king, with the soaring beauty of their proportions, the magnificence of the exotic collections they house, and their sheer size, second only to London's Kew Gardens.
The glasshouses in the Royal Domain of Laeken were designed as a conservatory for the members of the household to stroll and rest in, and they are sometimes used as a vast, fairytale reception room. King Baudouin receives his guests there, just as his great-great-uncle before him.

OUR HERITAGE LIVES ON

A country's history is written in its architecture: middle-class, provincial or industrial — it is always a synthesis of esthetic values and emotive force.

We in Belgium have often managed to protect our architectural heritage, restoring it tastefully or casting it in a new role. Examples of this — and there are thousands of them — can be seen in the Vandenhove houses in Liège, residences in Bruges, the 'Théâtre d'Hades' in Le Grand Hornu designed by the architect Henri Guchez.

ARCHITECTURE ON THE MOVE

Modern architecture sometimes takes the form of a temple of the future, or of a huge mirror reflecting the skies. Here we have the great hall of the Sart Tilman teaching hospital in Liège, and an office block — quite a speciality in Brussels, which is full of office blocks at very reasonable prices. The win-

dows, another Belgian speciality, show the reflection of one of these huge cranes which prove daily that Belgium is alive and growing.

Art of all kinds from all over the world finds a home here. The people of Belgium, stimulated by an education which has formed their artistic senses for at least 12 years, can browse through museums of all styles, both great and small, savouring the treasures they hold. Visitors from all corners of the world join them throughout the year, attracted by modern and classical collections, special exhibitions on a

grand scale, and the architectural setting, which is sometimes breathtaking. Right in the heart of our capital city, visitors can share a peep behind the scenes of a startling project: the finely-balanced facade of the Palace of Charles of Lorraine, now the Museum of Ancient Art, towers over the Museum of Modern Art, built underground beneath the old paving stones of the Square. It is open to the sky, already revealing some of its treasures to passers-by.

ART ON DISPLAY

Works of art are not only found in the museums. They are whisked from picture rails and pedestals to decorate metro stations and other public places. Or a whole crowd of them take off to spend a holiday in a series of beautiful private homes, where they adorn their 'guest rooms' and receive their admirers in

state. Such an event took place in Ghent in 1986, and many visitors came to enjoy this unique happening.

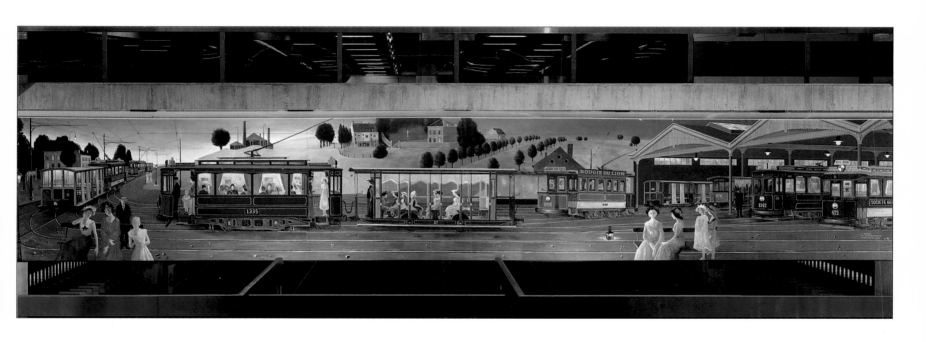

AVANT-GARDE THEATRE

Jan Fabre of Antwerp, who has become almost a permanent fixture at all the European festivals, took Londoners by surprise at the Royal Albert Hall with his nonconformist theatre presented as surrealistic tableaux. This actor and one-man-orchestra started his career with a one-man-show at the age of 17, and is now producing a trilogy of operas, with script, scenery, costumes, choreography and production all by Jan Fabre.

WOMAN OF THE YEAR

Marion Hänsel, a successful film producer, is seen here in action directing 'Les Noces barbares', after 'Le Lit' and 'Dust'.

A COMPETITION WHICH BEARS
A ROYAL NAME

A major event of the musical season,
the Queen Elisabeth International Music Competition has won its fame not
only through the active royal patronage
which it enjoys, but also because of the
very demanding level of the events,
their duration, the valuable prizes and

the reputation of the virtuosi and teachers who sit on the jury.

THE ENCHANTMENT OF THE THÉÂTRE ROYAL DE LA MONNAIE / KONINKLIJKE MUNTSCHOUWBURG

First built in 1700, the Théâtre de la Monnaie / Koninklijke Muntschouwburg has always been one of the temples of musical and theatrical life in Belgium.
Both classical and contemporary works

attract audiences from Belgium and even abroad.
Seated under a vast crystal chandelier, ballet and opera fans watch the red curtain go up on a stage transformed by scenery manipulated by the latest hi-tech machinery.

THE COUNTLESS VOICES OF THE CARILLONS

Each village and every quarter has its own belfry, pointing like a finger at the sky. Some belfries even house a whole orchestra of bells — and these are the famous carillons, renowned since the Middle Ages.

Every day, these carillons peal out in

Mechelen, Bruges, Brussels, Ath, Ghent, Louvain and many other cities in Belgium. Playing religious music, classical music, folk melodies or a potpourri of modern tunes, they enliven the town. Many a moment spent relaxing on the terrace of a café on the marketplace is thus turned into a festive event.

Master bell-ringers pit their skills in loud competition, and share their rare knowledge in a bell-ringing school of world fame: the Lemmensinstituut in Mechelen.

HISTORY TAKES TO THE STREETS

Although Belgians belong firmly to this day and age, and are deeply attached to their own firesides, they still love to come out onto the streets to watch their national history march past. The small screen has not replaced the traditional processions which once paraded through fields and villages, and our

streets still burst into colour as great historical events are relived, or tableaux vivants depicting scenes from the Scriptures roll past.

FROM CLASSICAL MUSIC TO JAZZ

Some are trained in the countless local music academies, practising everywhere, even in public places. Others are stars of international fame, like Toots Thielemans. America claims half of his time, with commissions to write film music, play his interpretation of great jazz compositions, or his own per-

sonal creations. Using quite simple instruments, a harmonica and a guitar simultaneously, he conjures up his own unique style of music, widely acclaimed by his bemused audiences.

The Torhout/Werchter Rockfestival in Flanders: a double-barrelled volley of decibels from the massed ranks of instruments and young people who have gathered together in Torhout near Bruges and Werchter near Louvain since 1977. The original 5,000 spectators have swelled to 120,000, and even

more fans would come if the organizers permitted. But Herman Schueremans has set a limit of 60,000 spectators for the Saturday and 60,000 on the Sunday of the first weekend in July, with an eye to comfort and safety. It's a long, hot weekend, with the sun or without, for a public taking a beating from brass and percussion, synthesizers and very electric guitars!

FEARSOME OR SMILING: THE GIANTS

No-one seems to know where these giants come from, though they live all over Belgium nowadays, well-integrated among the local population, and only emerging on high days and holidays. They gaze down from the heights on the crowds of merrymakers, whirling and dancing until the last lantern has gone out. Then they creep off to sleep for the rest of the year in the village hall or the local fire station... funny life these giants lead.

ALL THE COLOURS OF THE CARNIVAL

Carnival comes in all shapes and sizes in Belgium: processions and feasts, dancing and music and the streets full of laughter. There are carnivals in every season, and local traditions to go with them.

Lords and ladies in their dazzling costumes, peaceful citizens dressed up as soldiers of Napoleon, 'Blancs-Moussis' with long, red noses, men and women disguised as dragons or cats: every corner of Belgium can always find something to celebrate — mid-lent, a saint's day, the hop harvest, the grape harvest or whatever.

ANCIENT FESTIVITIES

Celebrated since the Middle Ages, the Carnival of Binche took on its unique character as we know it today around 1500, imitating the plumes and paintings of the Incas which Christopher Columbus brought back from America.

This picturesque interpretation comprises a costume embroidered with lions, lace, a hat decorated with ostrich feathers, a belt hung with cattle bells and clogs clacking in time with rhythmic dances. As 'Gilles' dances, he brandishes his 'ramon' or broom and throws oranges to the people, instead of the original bread and local fruit, as a symbol of joy shared. The rich detail and centuries-old customs of this ritual are handed down from father to son and perpetuated by the whole town.

BETWEEN WORK AND FESTIVITY, PEACE REIGNS

A calm sea and the tranquillity of a frozen canal or pond: peace reigns on the waters.

SPORT IN ALL ITS FACETS

Belgian sportsmen and women have distinguished themselves in many branches of sport including athletics, judo, cycling, billiards, motocross and football.

Amateurs, professionals and spectators abound in archery, or cross-country skiing, the Brussels marathon or the martial arts, even if they do not all beat records like Ingrid Berghmans, five times world champion judoka.

MEDICINE: A PROLIFIC SECTOR

The medical services are excellent in Belgium: the number of doctors, hospitals and pharmacists is well above the European average. The quality of medical care is as high as that of medical research. The teaching hospitals take on both tasks simultaneously and have done pioneering work in the field of

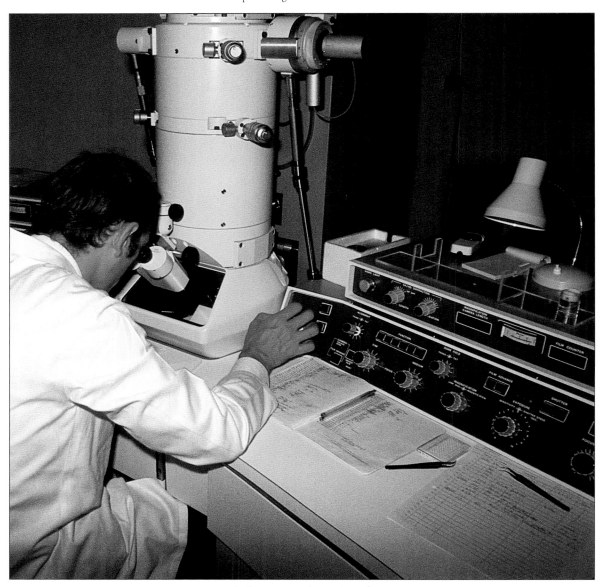

medical treatment and operating techniques.

Tropical medicine is one of our specialities, and the Institute of Tropical Medicine in Antwerp attracts students from all over the world.

Belgian doctors, agronomists, engineers, builders, teachers and missionaries have always offered to share knowledge with the world and offer their aid where needed.

This aid has been given in every continent, sometimes as a purely Belgian undertaking and sometimes in the context of the large-scale programmes drawn up mainly by UNO, FAO, UNESCO and the World Bank and its branches. A particular interest has been shown in Africa.

In addition to state action, there have also been initiatives from the universities proposing training schemes, scientific exchanges and the provision of material, and the dynamic action of the nongovernmental organizations. The latter, most of which depend largely on voluntary work, collect funds from the public to fund specific projects. Their spectacular success confirms with every campaign just how deeply the people of Belgium care about the problems of humanity.

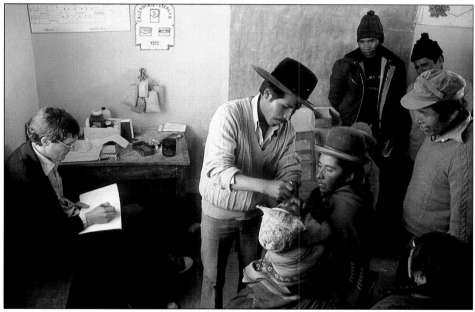

TRANSFER OF KNOWLEDGE

Belgians are actively involved in educational projects all over the world. Many third world students also come to Belgium to study at our universities and technical colleges or to undergo intensive training in Belgian industry.

SCIENTIFIC RESEARCH
IN CENTRAL AFRICA

In the Museum built for Léopold II in Tervuren at the beginning of the century by the French architect who had also designed the Petit Palais in Paris, Léopold centralised the study of an astonishing range of collections, and the collections themselves, all on the

subject of the human sciences, natural sciences and agricultural and mining products from Africa. The work of this scientific institute has continued steadily ever since, with fieldwork carried out in cooperation with African researchers.

203

THEY'RE ALL DIFFERENT, AND THEY'RE ALL BELGIAN

With their feet on the ground and their heads in the clouds, serious bons-vivants, peaceable and yet active, pensive and audacious, flexible and tenacious, reserved and warm-hearted: the people of Belgium combine northern

vigour with southern vivacity, a deep love of their country and an openness towards Europe and the world.

ACKNOWLEDGEMENTS ARE MADE
TO THE FOLLOWING PERSONS,
INSTITUTIONS AND COMPANIES
WHO HAVE ASSISTED THE
PUBLISHERS AND PHOTOGRAPHERS
IN THE COLLECTION OF THE
ICONOGRAPHIC MATERIAL

ACEC SA
Agfa-Gevaert
Artois NV
Barco Electronic NV
Bekaert NV
Belgisch Instituut voor Voorlichting en
Documentatie / Institut Belge
d'Information et de Documentation
Bell Telephone MFG Co NV
B.N. Spoorwegmaterieel en
metaalconstructies NV
Prof. Pierre Boone
CMB NV-SA
Daf-Trucks NV
De Coene-Construct NV
De Poortere SA
Dossche NV
Fabrique Nationale Herstal (FN) SA
Faculté des sciences agronomiques de
l'Etat à Gembloux
Café Le Fallstaf
Fashion Fashion
Gemeente Gavere, Brandweerkorps
Société Générale de Banque SA /
Generale Bankmaatschappij NV
Marion Hansel
Ial Space-Université de Liège
Instituut voor Tropische Geneeskunde
Prins Leopold / Institut de Médecine
Tropical Prince Léopold
Interuniversity Micro-Electronics
Center v.z.w.
Janssens Pharmaceutica NV
Jonckheere (Carrosseriebouw) PVBA
Katholiek Documentatie- en
Onderzoekscentrum
Octave Landuyt
Maatschappij voor Brugse
Zeevaartinrichtingen NV
Hôtel Métropole SA Brussel / Bruxelles
Mietec NV
Ministère des Travaux Publics /
Ministerie van Openbare Werken
Het Museum van de Dynastie v.z.w. /
Le Musée de la Dynastie a.s.b.l.
Office National des Débouchés
Agricoles et Horticoles / Nationale
Dienst voor Afzet van Land- en
Tuinbouwprodukten

Nationaal Instituut voor
Radio-elementen / Institut National des
Radioéléments (I.R.E.)
Société Nationale des Chemins de fer
Belges / Nationale Maatschappij voor
Belgische Spoorwegen
Oip Optics NV
Phenix Works SA
Plant Genetic Systems NV
Prado NV
Provinciaal Instituut voor Hoger
Onderwijs Gent
Public Relations Partners SA / NV
Regie van Telegrafie en Telefonie /
Régie des Télégraphes et des
Téléphones
Rijksdienst voor Arbeidsvoorziening te
Oudenaarde
Sabena NV / SA
SCHAAMTe v.z.w.
Sidmar NV
Société Nationale de Construction
Aérospatiale (SONACA) SA
De stad Antwerpen, Hugo Leon Morales
'Les Cyclistes'
Stichting Ons Erfdeel, v.z.w.
Troubleyn v.z.w.
UCO NV
Vlaams Commissariaat-Generaal voor
Toerisme
Het Volk NV
Volvo Europa Car NV
Windmasters H.M.Z. - Belgium NV
Monsieur et madame Wittamer
l'Hôpital Brugmann à Bruxelles /
Ziekenhuis Brugmann te Brussel

SOURCES OF THE PHOTOGRAPHS

Yann Arthus-Bertrand / Travel Pictures:
p. 131
Barsamian: p. 126
Christine Bastin, Jacques Evrard: p. 24,
26, 27, 43, 60, 78, 79, 82, 86a, 86b, 88,
92, 93, 94, 96, 97, 103, 108, 112a,
115a, 115b, 118, 124, 129b, 150, 152,
157, 170, 172, 174b, 175, 176, 178a,
178b, 179, 192a, 192b, 193, 196b,
196d, 197b, 203, 204c, 204j, 204l,
205a, 205c, 205d, 205e, 205j, 205k
Bell Telephone: p. 117, 164a
Dirk Buwalda: p. 90
Christiaen Carez: p. 112b, 199
Caroline Info-PRP: p. 204g
Paul Coerten: p. 106b, 127, 132
Christian De Bruyne / Travel Pictures:
p. 159, 196a
Fotogravure De Buck: p. 116
Jan Decreton: p. 69, 87, 95, 160, 195
Marie-Laure De Decker / Photo News:
p. 67
M. Deville / Photo News: p. 48, 164b
S. Domelounksen / Travel Pictures:
p. 145a, 149
European Parliament: p. 164a
Fashion Fashion: p. 137, 204a
Generale Bankmaatschappij / Société
Générale de Banque: p. 168, 169
Anne Ginetti: p. 184
M. Gouverneur / Photo news: p. 196c
Marion Hansel: p. 183
Michiel Hendryckx: p. 76
Ial-Space: p. 128
Instituut voor Tropische Geneeskunde:
p. 198
Janssens Pharmaceutica: p. 133b
KADOC: p. 46
Peter Labarque: p. 101, 111, 120a,
120b, 121a, 121b, 129a, 134, 146a, 167
Claude Levesque: p. 80, 91,105, 106a,
114, 122, 130, 135, 141, 186a, 186b,
197a
Joris Luyten: p. 41
Charles Mahaux / Photo News: p. 16
M.B.Z., Henderyckx: p. 147b
C. Michel / Travel Pictures: p. 142
Ministère des Travaux Public /

Ministerie van Openbare Werken:
p. 139a, 139b
Louis Moeyersoms: p. 205b
Museum voor de Dynastie / Musée de la
Dynastie: p. 42, 47
O.N.D.A.H. / N.D.A.L.T.P.: p. 102
Paul Peeters: p. 190, 205f
Guy Phillipart de Foy / Travel Pictures:
p. 194
Photo news: p. 16, 18, 29, 64
Benoit Roland / Travel Pictures: p. 185
Jean-Jacques Rousseau: p. 40, 113, 161,
166, 181, 187
Jean-Jacques Rousseau, Travel Pictures:
p. 110
Sabena: p. 148
Sidmar, Vandenberghe: p. 30
Yves Smets / Photo News: p. 74
Herman Sorgeloos / SCHAAMTe v.z.w.:
p. 70
Troubleyn v.z.w.: p. 182
UCO: p. 202b
Valeer Vanbekbergen: p. 165
Van den Eeckhoudt: p. 125, 177
Michel Vanneuville: p. 53, 62, 189,
204h
Philip Vanoutrive: p. 2, 22, 31, 32, 38,
45, 52, 56, 58, 59, 68, 76, 84, 85, 89,
98, 100, 104, 107, 112c, 119, 133a,
136, 138a, 138b, 143, 144a, 144b,
145b, 146b, 147a, 154, 156, 162, 174a,
180, 188a, 188b, 204b, 204d, 204e,
204f, 204i, 204j, 205g, 205i
P.-H. Versele / Photo News: p. 163,
205k
Vlaams Commissariaat-Generaal voor
Toerisme: p. 153
Henri-Louis Weichselbaum: p. 73, 155,
191, 207
Wereldwijd / Robert D'Hoe: p. 200a,
200b, 201a, 201b, 202a
Wilkin / Travel Pictures: p. 54
Wittamer: p. 171